101 THINGS® TO DO WITH

PORK

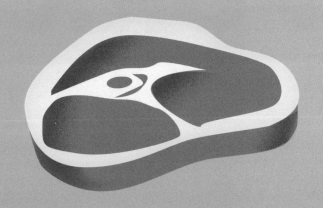

101 THINGS® TO DO WITH

PORK

ELIZA CROSS

Gibbs Smith

First Edition
29 28 27 26 25   5 4 3 2 1

Published by
Gibbs Smith
570 N. Sportsplex Dr.
Kaysville, Utah 84037

1.800.835.4993 orders
www.gibbs-smith.com

Designed by Ryan Thomann and Renee Bond
Printed and bound in China

Library of Congress Control Number: 2024950966
ISBN: 978-1-4236-6853-4
Ebook ISBN: 978-1-4236-6854-1

This product is made of FSC®-certified and other controlled material.

MIX
Paper | Supporting
responsible forestry
FSC® C144853

For Aunt Edie Schmidt

CONTENTS

Helpful Hints

- To avoid cross contamination, use one cutting board for raw pork and a separate one for fresh produce.

- Using an instant-read thermometer is the best way to ensure accurate doneness for pork. When a range of time is included, check on the early side and adjust accordingly.

- According to the National Pork Board, the safe internal cooking temperature for fresh cuts of pork (like chops and tenderloin) is 145 degrees F, and 160 degrees F for ground pork.

- For larger cuts of pork that will be cut into slices, like a roast, rest the meat for 10 minutes before carving to allow juices to be distributed.

- Store cooked pork, tightly covered or wrapped, in the coldest part of the refrigerator and plan to use within 3 days.

- To freeze pork, make sure it is completely cooled first. Wrap the meat tightly in freezer-safe wrap, in a freezer bag, or freezer-safe container. Label with the date, and plan to use within 2 months.

- For best results when thawing frozen pork, transfer the package or container to the refrigerator and allow it to slowly thaw for 12 hours.

- For detailed information about cooking pork, visit: www.pork.org/pork-cooking-temperature.

Recipe Notes

- The recipes in this book were tested with large eggs and all-purpose flour.

- If a particular ingredient is not specified, such as salted or unsalted butter, you can use whichever you like and adjust the seasonings accordingly.

- When the recipe specifies fine sea salt, you may substitute table salt in the same quantity.

- Kosher salt crystals are larger and coarser than fine sea salt crystals. To substitute kosher salt for fine sea salt, use $1\frac{1}{4}$ teaspoons kosher salt in place of 1 teaspoon fine sea salt.

- Sea salt tends to taste saltier than kosher salt. To substitute fine sea salt for kosher salt, use $\frac{3}{4}$ teaspoon fine sea salt in place of 1 teaspoon kosher salt.

- It's best to under-salt slightly when substituting fine sea salt for kosher salt, and taste. You can always add a bit more salt, if needed.

BREAKFAST
&
BRUNCH

Sausage and Green Chile Breakfast Burritos

MAKES 8 SERVINGS

12 ounces	bulk breakfast sausage
½	medium yellow onion, chopped
1 can (4 ounces)	diced green chiles, undrained
1 tablespoon	butter
1 tablespoon	extra-virgin olive oil
2	large potatoes, peeled and cut into ½-inch dice
8	eggs, beaten
1½ cups	shredded cheddar cheese, divided
8	flour tortillas, warmed
	kosher salt and freshly ground black pepper, to taste
1 cup	salsa

Cook the sausage in a large frying pan over medium heat, breaking up with a spatula, until browned, about 8 minutes. Drain on paper towels and crumble when cooled; set aside.

Return the frying pan to the stove and add the chopped onion to the sausage drippings. Cook over medium heat until onion is tender, stirring occasionally, about 5 minutes. Add the green chiles and cook until hot and bubbling, 1–2 minutes. Cool and transfer to a large bowl.

Wipe out the frying pan and heat the butter and olive oil over medium heat until the butter melts. Add the potatoes and cook, turning occasionally, until golden brown. Transfer the potatoes to the bowl, leaving the drippings in the frying pan. Return the frying pan to the stove and turn heat to medium-low. Add the eggs and cook, stirring, just until scrambled.

Add the eggs to the bowl along with the reserved sausage. Add 1 cup cheese and stir gently until ingredients are combined.

Spoon ⅛ of the filling in the center of each warm tortilla and sprinkle with 1 tablespoon cheese. Season to taste with salt and pepper. Roll each burrito up tightly and serve with salsa.

#2
Bacon and Cheddar Quiche
MAKES 6 SERVINGS

1	refrigerated pie crust
6 slices	bacon, crisply cooked and crumbled
1 cup	shredded sharp cheddar cheese
4	eggs
1 cup	half-and-half
¼ teaspoon	fine sea salt
¼ teaspoon	freshly ground black pepper

Preheat oven to 375 degrees F.

Press the refrigerated pie crust into a 9-inch pie dish. Sprinkle cooked bacon and cheese evenly over the crust.

In a medium mixing bowl, whisk together eggs, half-and-half, salt, and pepper. Pour the egg mixture over the bacon and cheese in the pie crust.

Bake for 35–40 minutes, or until the center is set and the top is golden brown. Let it cool for 5 minutes before cutting in wedges and serving.

Pork Lovers' Breakfast Skillet

MAKES 6 SERVINGS

6	eggs
⅓ cup	half-and-half
½ pound	bacon, chopped
½ pound	bulk breakfast sausage
2 tablespoons	butter
2	medium russet potatoes, peeled and diced
½ teaspoon	kosher salt
¼ teaspoon	freshly ground black pepper
¼ cup	finely chopped onion
¼ pound	diced cooked ham
½ cup	shredded cheddar cheese

In a small bowl, whisk together the eggs and half-and-half; set aside.

Heat a large frying pan over medium heat. Add bacon and cook until crisp. Remove and drain on paper towels. Pour the bacon grease from the pan (save for cooking or discard) and wipe out the frying pan.

Add the sausage and cook, breaking up with the spatula, until lightly browned, about 8 minutes. Drain on paper towels and crumble. Wipe out the frying pan, add butter, and cook over medium heat until it foams. Add the potatoes, salt, and pepper, and cook, stirring occasionally, until tender and golden, about 10 minutes. Stir in the onion and cook until tender, about 4 minutes. Add the bacon, sausage, and ham, and cook, stirring occasionally, for 2 minutes. Add the egg mixture and stir until the eggs are almost cooked but still moist, 3–4 minutes. Sprinkle with cheddar cheese and cook, stirring gently, until cheese is melted, about 1 more minute. Serve hot.

Maple Bacon French Toast

MAKES 8 SERVINGS

1 pound	maple-flavored sliced bacon
8 ounces	cream cheese, softened
1$\frac{1}{4}$ cups	dark brown sugar, packed
$\frac{1}{2}$ teaspoon	maple extract
$\frac{1}{8}$ teaspoon	fine sea salt
1 loaf (16 slices)	thin-sliced bread
6	eggs
$\frac{1}{3}$ cup	milk
2 tablespoons	butter, plus extra for topping
1 tablespoon	vegetable oil
	pure maple syrup, for drizzling

Cook the bacon in a frying pan over medium heat until browned and crispy. Drain on paper towels. When cool, break each piece in thirds and set aside.

In a medium bowl, combine the cream cheese, brown sugar, maple extract, and salt, and stir until blended. Spread the mixture on each of the 16 bread slices. Divide the bacon pieces evenly among 8 of the bread slices and top with remaining 8 bread slices, filling-side down.

In a shallow dish, whisk together the eggs and milk. Heat the butter and oil in a large frying pan or griddle over medium heat until the butter melts and oil shimmers. Dip the French toast sandwiches quickly in the egg mixture and cook in the frying pan, browning both sides, about 6 minutes total. Serve hot with butter and maple syrup.

#5

Cheesy Sausage Biscuits

MAKES 10 SERVINGS

8 ounces	**bulk pork breakfast sausage**
1 tube (12 ounces, 10-count)	**refrigerated buttermilk biscuits**
2	**eggs**
1/8 teaspoon	**fine sea salt**
1/8 teaspoon	**freshly ground black pepper**
1/2 cup	**shredded cheddar cheese**
1 1/2 tablespoons	**finely chopped fresh chives or green onions**

Preheat oven to 400 degrees F and lightly grease a 12-cup muffin pan.

Brown the sausage in a large frying pan over medium heat, breaking up with a spatula, until cooked and browned. Cool on paper towels and crumble; set aside.

On a lightly floured work surface, roll out each biscuit in a 5-inch circle. Press each biscuit in the cup of the muffin pan. Divide the sausage among the cups.

In a small bowl, whisk together the eggs, salt, and pepper. Stir in the cheese, and spoon the mixture into cups, dividing equally. Sprinkle with chives. Bake until eggs are set and biscuit edges are lightly browned, 12–15 minutes. Cool for 5 minutes and remove from pan.

#6
Ham and Cheese Breakfast Turnovers

MAKES 8 SERVINGS

1 sheet	frozen puff pastry dough, thawed (from a 17.3-ounce package)
8 teaspoons	mild prepared mustard
8 slices	sharp cheddar cheese
16 thin deli slices	Black Forest ham
1	egg
1 tablespoon	water

Preheat oven to 425 degrees F. Fit a piece of parchment paper in a baking sheet.

Move the parchment paper to a flat work surface and roll out the puff pastry dough in a rectangle.

Using a pizza cutter or sharp knife, cut the dough in 8 equal rectangles. Slide the parchment paper with the pastry rectangles back on the baking sheet.

Spread 1 teaspoon mustard evenly on each of the rectangles. Top with a slice of cheese followed by 2 ham slices. Pull the top left corner down to the center and then overlap it with the opposite corner on the bottom right. Seal the edges of the pastry by pinching together tightly. Repeat the process for all the puff pastry turnovers.

In a small bowl, whisk together the egg and water. Using a pastry brush, brush the egg wash on top of each turnover. Bake the turnovers in the preheated oven until the cheese melts and the pastry is golden brown, about 15 minutes.

Ham and Cheese Hash Brown Casserole

MAKES 10 SERVINGS

1 can (10.5 ounces)	condensed cream of chicken soup
1 container (8 ounces)	sour cream
1/2 cup	butter, melted
1/2 teaspoon	freshly ground black pepper
1/4 teaspoon	fine sea salt
1 bag (32 ounces)	frozen shredded hash brown potatoes, thawed
2 cups	shredded sharp cheddar cheese, divided
8 ounces	cooked, diced ham

Preheat oven to 350 degrees F and grease a 9 x 13-inch baking dish.

In a large bowl, combine the soup, sour cream, butter, pepper, and salt until well blended. Add the hash browns, 1 1/2 cups cheese, and ham, and stir well. Spread evenly into the prepared dish and sprinkle with the remaining 1/2 cup cheese.

Bake until bubbly and lightly brown on top, about 1 hour. Cool for 5 minutes. Cut into squares and serve.

Chorizo Scrambled Eggs

MAKES 4 SERVINGS

1 tablespoon	vegetable oil
½ pound	chorizo, crumbled
½	sweet yellow onion, finely chopped
2 cloves	garlic, minced
1	medium tomato, chopped
6	eggs, beaten
¼ teaspoon	fine sea salt
¼ teaspoon	freshly ground black pepper
⅓ cup	pico de gallo or salsa
1	ripe avocado, peeled and diced

Heat oil in a large frying pan over medium-high heat until it shimmers. Add the chorizo and cook until lightly browned, stirring occasionally, about 6 minutes.

Reduce heat to medium and add the onion. Cook, stirring occasionally, until the onion is translucent. Add the garlic and tomato and cook, stirring occasionally, for 4 minutes. Add the eggs, salt, and pepper, and continue cooking, stirring occasionally, until the eggs are cooked, about 4 minutes.

Divide among four plates, drizzle with pico de gallo, and top with chopped avocado.

Sausage-and-Waffle Bake

MAKES 8 SERVINGS

1 pound	maple breakfast sausage links
8	fresh or frozen toasted waffles
1½ cups	shredded Colby Jack cheese
1¼ cups	milk
8	eggs
½ cup	pure maple syrup, plus additional for drizzling

Preheat oven to 375 degrees F and lightly grease a 9 x 13-inch baking dish.

In a frying pan over medium heat, cook the sausage until lightly browned and fully cooked, 8–10 minutes. Drain on paper towels and cut links into ½-inch slices.

Cut the waffles into 1½-inch squares and arrange in the baking dish. Arrange the sausage pieces on top and sprinkle with the cheese.

In a medium bowl, combine the milk, eggs, and maple syrup and whisk to blend. Drizzle over the sausage mixture. Bake until golden brown and cooked through, 45–50 minutes. Cut into squares and serve with additional maple syrup on the side.

Maple Sausage Pancake Sandwiches

MAKES 6 SERVINGS

12 ounces	maple breakfast sausage
12	medium pancakes (homemade or store-bought)
2 tablespoons	butter, softened
2 tablespoons	pure maple syrup

Form the breakfast sausage into 6 round patties, each about ¼ inch thick. In a large frying pan over medium heat, cook the sausage patties on both sides until browned, 9–10 minutes. Remove from the heat and drain patties on paper towels.

To warm pancakes, heat the oven to 350 degrees F and arrange pancakes on a baking sheet in a single layer. Cover pan with a sheet of aluminum foil, and bake until pancakes are warm, 5–6 minutes.

In a small bowl, mash together the butter and maple syrup with a spoon until combined.

To assemble sandwiches, spread one side of all the pancakes with the maple butter. Arrange sausage patties on 6 of the pancakes, and top with the remaining 6 pancakes, maple butter–side down. Serve warm.

Pulled Pork Breakfast Tacos

MAKES 6 SERVINGS

¼ cup	chopped tomato
¼ cup	chopped onion
1	large Anaheim pepper, seeded and finely chopped
1	small ripe avocado, chopped
2 teaspoons	fresh lime juice
1½ cups	chopped leftover pulled pork*
2 tablespoons	butter
6	eggs, beaten
	kosher salt and freshly ground black pepper, to taste
6	flour tortillas, warmed
½ cup	shredded Monterey Jack cheese
	salsa, sour cream, and chopped cilantro, for serving

In a small bowl, combine the tomato, onion, Anaheim pepper, avocado, and lime juice and stir gently to blend; set aside.

Reheat the pork in a saucepan over medium heat, stirring occasionally, until hot, about 5 minutes. Cover and keep warm.

Heat the butter in a large frying pan over medium heat until it foams. Add the eggs and cook, stirring, just until scrambled. Remove from the heat and season with salt and pepper.

To assemble tacos, divide the pork among the six tortillas. Top with scrambled eggs and the tomato-avocado mixture. Sprinkle with cheese and fold gently in half. Serve with salsa, sour cream, and chopped cilantro.

*See page 97 for Perfect Pulled Pork recipe.

Bratwurst and Swiss Omelet

MAKES 2 SERVINGS

2	cooked bratwurst or German sausage links, cut into ¼-inch slices
6	eggs
¼ cup	water
¼ teaspoon	fine sea salt
¼ teaspoon	freshly ground black pepper
1 tablespoon	butter
1 cup	shredded Swiss cheese chopped chives or green onions (green part only), for garnish

In a medium nonstick frying pan over medium heat, cook the bratwurst slices until lightly browned, turning once, 5–6 minutes. Wipe out the frying pan and drain bratwurst slices on paper towels.

Combine the eggs, water, salt, and pepper in a medium mixing bowl and whisk to blend.

Return the frying pan to the stove and melt the butter over medium heat. Add the egg mixture, spread it with a spatula, and swirl until it begins to set, about 3 minutes. Add the sausage slices and sprinkle the cheese evenly over the eggs. Cook for 2 more minutes. Use a spatula to carefully fold the omelet in half and cook for 1 minute more, or until eggs are done. Slide the omelet onto a serving plate and cut in half. Sprinkle with chives and serve.

Bacon and Cheese Breakfast Sliders

MAKES 12 SLIDERS

1 package (12-count)	sweet Hawaiian rolls
10	eggs
½ teaspoon	seasoning salt
¼ teaspoon	freshly ground black pepper
3 tablespoons	butter, melted, divided
1½ ounces	cream cheese, cubed
12 strips	crispy cooked bacon, broken in thirds
6 slices	Colby Jack cheese
2 tablespoons	grated Parmesan cheese
	finely chopped chives, for garnish

Preheat oven to 350 degrees F and lightly grease the bottom of a 9 x 13-inch glass baking dish.

Cut the Hawaiian rolls in half horizontally and put the bottom half of the rolls in the prepared baking dish.

Combine the eggs, seasoning salt, and pepper in a medium bowl, and whisk until well combined.

In a large nonstick frying pan over medium heat, add 1 tablespoon melted butter. Add the egg mixture and cook for several minutes, until curds start to form. Stir gently with a spatula and scatter the cubes of cream cheese over the eggs. Continue cooking, lifting the eggs with the spatula and gently incorporating the cream cheese, until the eggs are just cooked.

Remove from the heat and use a slotted spoon to evenly layer the eggs over the bottom buns.

Arrange the bacon pieces over the eggs so that each bun has 3 pieces of bacon. Top with the cheese slices, followed by the top buns. Brush with remaining melted butter, cover with aluminum foil, and bake for 10 minutes. Remove foil and continue baking until the cheese is melted and buns are golden brown, about 10 more minutes. Cool for 5 minutes and cut into individual sliders using a sharp knife. Sprinkle with Parmesan cheese and chopped chives.

Canadian Bacon Breakfast Pizza

MAKES 8 SERVINGS

1 tube (13.8 ounces)	refrigerated pizza crust or 3/4-pound ball prepared pizza dough
1 1/2 tablespoons	extra-virgin olive oil, divided
6 ounces	sliced Canadian bacon
6	eggs
1/4 cup	milk
1 tablespoon	butter
2 cups	shredded Colby Jack cheese kosher salt and freshly ground black pepper, to taste

Preheat oven to 400 degrees F and grease a 10 x 15-inch baking pan.

Unroll and press dough in the bottom of the prepared pan. Prick thoroughly with a fork and brush with 1 tablespoon oil. Bake until lightly browned, 7–8 minutes.

While crust is baking, cut each of the Canadian bacon rounds in 6 wedge-shaped pieces. Brush a large nonstick frying pan with remaining 1/2 tablespoon oil and cook the Canadian bacon over medium heat, turning occasionally, until cooked through and just starting to brown, about 6 minutes. Drain on paper towels; set aside. Wipe out the frying pan.

In a medium bowl, whisk together eggs and milk. Heat the butter in the frying pan over medium heat until it foams. Add eggs; cook and stir just until thickened. Spoon eggs over pizza crust. Arrange Canadian bacon over the top and sprinkle with cheese. Bake until cheese is melted, 5–7 minutes. Sprinkle with salt and pepper, cut into 8 pieces, and serve.

Italian Sausage Scramble

MAKES 4 SERVINGS

1 tablespoon	extra-virgin olive oil
½ pound	cooked Italian sausage links, cut into ¼-inch slices
1	large tomato, chopped
1 cup	baby spinach leaves, firmly packed
8	eggs, beaten
½ teaspoon	kosher salt
¼ teaspoon	freshly ground black pepper
4	large fresh basil leaves, finely chopped, divided
⅓ cup	shredded mozzarella cheese

Heat the oil in a large frying pan over medium heat. Add the sausage slices and cook, stirring occasionally, until lightly browned, about 5 minutes. Add the tomato and cook, stirring, about 1 minute.

Reduce the heat to medium-low and add the spinach. Cook until wilted, about 3 minutes. Push the spinach to the side of the pan and add the eggs, salt, and pepper. Cook, stirring occasionally, until eggs are set, 4–5 minutes. Mix with the spinach and add half of the basil. Cook for 1 more minute, remove from the heat, and immediately sprinkle evenly with the mozzarella cheese. Rest for 5 minutes to allow the cheese to melt. Divide mixture among four plates and sprinkle with the remaining half of the chopped basil.

Crustless Spinach and Sausage Quiche

MAKES 6 SERVINGS

½ pound	bulk breakfast sausage
1 cup	fresh baby spinach leaves
6	eggs
1 cup	shredded mozzarella cheese
½ cup	milk
¼ teaspoon	fine sea salt
¼ teaspoon	freshly ground black pepper

Preheat oven to 350 degrees F and lightly grease a 9-inch glass pie dish.

In a medium frying pan over medium heat, cook the sausage until browned. Drain excess grease. Add spinach to the frying pan and cook until wilted, about 2 minutes. Remove pan from heat and set aside.

In a medium bowl, whisk together eggs, cheese, milk, salt, and pepper. Add the sausage and spinach mixture and stir well. Pour in prepared pie dish. Bake until the quiche is lightly browned around the edges and set in the center, 30–35 minutes. Cool for 5 minutes before cutting in wedges and serving.

Kielbasa Potato Skillet

MAKES 4 SERVINGS

2 tablespoons	extra-virgin olive oil
4	medium russet potatoes, peeled and diced
1	small onion, chopped
1 pound	kielbasa, cut into $\frac{1}{4}$-inch slices
$\frac{1}{2}$ teaspoon	kosher salt
$\frac{1}{4}$ teaspoon	freshly ground black pepper
$\frac{1}{2}$ teaspoon	smoked or regular paprika chopped fresh parsley, for garnish

In a large frying pan, heat the oil over medium heat until it shimmers. Add the diced potatoes and cook, stirring occasionally, until lightly golden and tender, 10–12 minutes.

Add the chopped onion and kielbasa to the frying pan and cook, stirring frequently, until the onion is soft and the kielbasa is browned, about 5 minutes. Season with salt, pepper, and paprika. Remove from the heat, garnish with chopped parsley, and serve hot.

Overnight Eggs Benedict Bake
MAKES 6 SERVINGS

6	English muffins, split and toasted
8 ounces	sliced Canadian bacon
8	eggs
2 cups	milk
½ teaspoon	fine sea salt
¼ teaspoon	pepper
1 cup	hollandaise sauce, prepared or homemade
	fresh chives, for garnish

Grease a 9 x 13-inch baking dish. Layer toasted English muffins in the pan. Cut the Canadian bacon in 1-inch slices and layer evenly over the English muffins.

In a bowl, whisk together eggs, milk, salt, and pepper. Pour the mixture over the muffins and bacon. Cover and refrigerate overnight.

The next morning, preheat oven to 350 degrees F. Bake uncovered for 40–45 minutes, or until the eggs are set. Warm the hollandaise sauce in a small saucepan over medium-low heat, and drizzle it over the casserole. Garnish with fresh chives. Cut into squares and serve warm.

SANDWICHES

Pork Sandwiches with Crispy Slaw

MAKES 8 SERVINGS

⅓ cup	mayonnaise
2 tablespoons	dill or sweet pickle juice
1½ teaspoons	apple cider vinegar
1 teaspoon	sugar
⅛ teaspoon	fine sea salt
¼ teaspoon	freshly ground black pepper
¼ teaspoon	dry mustard
1	medium dill pickle, finely chopped (about 2 tablespoons)
1 tablespoon	finely chopped onion
2 cups	bagged coleslaw mix
2⅔ cups	chopped pulled pork*
½ cup	barbecue sauce
8	large onion buns, split and toasted

In a large bowl, whisk together the mayonnaise, pickle juice, vinegar, sugar, salt, pepper, and mustard until smooth. Add the pickle, onion, and coleslaw mix, and toss with a fork to combine.

In a large nonstick frying pan, heat the pulled pork over medium heat and drizzle with the barbecue sauce. Cook, stirring frequently, until mixture just starts to bubble. Divide the pulled pork among the bottom buns. Top with coleslaw and the top buns.

*See page 97 for Perfect Pulled Pork recipe.

Cuban Sandwiches

MAKES 4 SERVINGS

	extra-virgin olive oil, for brushing
4	soft hoagie rolls, split
2 tablespoons	butter, softened
1 tablespoon	prepared yellow mustard
4	large dill pickles, sliced lengthwise
1 pound	thinly sliced roast pork
8 strips	bacon, cooked and drained
$\frac{1}{2}$ pound	thinly sliced ham
$\frac{1}{2}$ pound	sliced Swiss cheese

Brush a cast-iron frying pan, griddle, or double-sided sandwich maker lightly with oil and heat to medium.

Spread the outside of each roll with butter and the cut side with mustard. Layer each sandwich with pickles, pork, bacon, ham, and cheese.

Arrange sandwiches in pan (cook in batches, if necessary) and press down on the sandwich with a heavy frying pan or bacon press to flatten.

Grill the sandwiches until bread is golden brown and cheese is melted, 2–3 minutes per side or about 4 minutes total in a sandwich maker. Cut in half diagonally and serve.

Louisiana Pork Sliders

MAKES 12 SERVINGS

2 (about 1 pound each)	pork tenderloins, trimmed
2 teaspoons	vegetable oil
2 tablespoons	paprika
2 teaspoons	dried oregano
1½ teaspoons	garlic powder
½ teaspoon	freshly ground black pepper
½ teaspoon	kosher salt
½ teaspoon	ground cumin
¼ teaspoon	cayenne pepper
24	slider buns, split
	mayonnaise, for spreading
½	head iceberg lettuce, thinly sliced
1	medium red bell pepper, seeds removed, thinly sliced

Lightly grease a 9 x 13-inch baking dish. Brush the tenderloins all over with the vegetable oil. In a small bowl, whisk together the paprika, oregano, garlic powder, black pepper, salt, cumin, and cayenne. Sprinkle the mixture evenly all over the tenderloins. Arrange in the baking dish, cover, and refrigerate for at least 4 hours or overnight.

Preheat oven to 425 degrees F. Cook the tenderloins until a thermometer reads 160 degrees F, 30–40 minutes. Remove from the oven, cool, and cut into thin slices.

Spread the insides of the buns with mayonnaise. Top each of the bottom buns with some of the pork, lettuce, bell pepper slices, and top buns.

Grilled Pork and Bacon Burgers

MAKES 4 SERVINGS

6 strips	regular sliced bacon, chopped
1 clove	garlic, minced
1 pound	ground pork
1/2 teaspoon	kosher salt
1/4 teaspoon	freshly ground black pepper
	peanut or canola oil, for brushing
4 slices	cheddar cheese
4	sesame seed hamburger buns, split
	burger toppings such as sliced tomatoes, onions, pickles, mayonnaise, ketchup, and mustard

Preheat the grill to medium-high.

In the bowl of a food processor, pulse the bacon and garlic until coarsely ground and transfer to a large bowl. Add the ground pork, salt, and pepper and mix (using your hands, if necessary) until well combined. Form the mixture in 4 patties about 3/4 inch thick.

Brush the grill lightly with peanut oil. Arrange the burgers on the grill and cook until browned, 4–5 minutes. Gently flip over and continue cooking until browned and an instant-read thermometer measures 160 degrees F, 4–5 more minutes. Transfer the burgers to a large plate and immediately top with cheese slices. Lay the buns cut-side down on the grill and cook until lightly toasted, about 1 minute. Serve the burgers on the buns with toppings on the side.

Pork Chop Sandwiches

MAKES 4 SERVINGS

³/₄ cup	cornmeal
1 cup	flour
½ teaspoon	garlic powder
½ teaspoon	onion powder
½ teaspoon	dry mustard
½ teaspoon	paprika
1 cup	milk
4 (3-ounce)	thin boneless pork loin chops
½ teaspoon	kosher salt
¼ teaspoon	freshly ground black pepper
	peanut or canola oil, for frying
4	sesame hamburger buns, split and toasted
	prepared mustard, for spreading
	mayonnaise, for spreading
12	thin pickle slices
½ cup	shredded iceberg lettuce

Place cornmeal in a shallow bowl. In another shallow bowl, whisk together flour, garlic powder, onion powder, mustard, and paprika. Add milk and stir just until combined; set aside.

Using a meat mallet or rolling pin, pound chops to a thickness of about ¼ inch. Sprinkle with salt and pepper.

Pour oil to a depth of ½ inch in a large heavy frying pan, and heat over medium heat until it shimmers. Dip chops in cornmeal, lightly coating both sides. Dip in the batter, letting excess drip off, and carefully place in the frying pan, working in batches if needed. Cook, turning over once halfway during cooking, until internal temperature measures 145 degrees F on an instant-read thermometer and golden brown, about 4 minutes on each side. Drain on paper towels.

Spread the inner bun bottoms with mustard and the inner tops with mayonnaise. Place one pork chop on each bun bottom. Top with pickles, lettuce, and bun tops.

#24

I Love Pork Sandwiches
MAKES 4 SERVINGS

2 cups	chopped pulled pork, warmed*
4	sesame hamburger buns, split and toasted
8 slices	thick-cut bacon, cooked and drained, halved
½ pound	shaved ham, warmed
½ cup	barbecue sauce, warmed

Divide the pulled pork among the hamburger bun bottoms. Top each sandwich with 4 half-pieces of bacon. Evenly divide the ham among the sandwiches. Drizzle 2 tablespoons barbecue sauce over the ham. Cover each sandwich with the top bun and serve.

*See page 97 for Perfect Pulled Pork recipe.

Italian Sausage–Mozzarella Subs

MAKES 4 SERVINGS

4 (4-ounce)	Italian sausage links
¼ cup	water
1 tablespoon	extra-virgin olive oil
1	medium onion, thinly sliced
1	medium green bell pepper, thinly sliced
1 clove	garlic, minced
1 cup	marinara sauce
4	brat buns, split and toasted
¼ cup	shredded mozzarella cheese

Place sausages and water in a large frying pan over high heat; bring to a boil. Reduce heat to medium-low; cover and simmer for 10 minutes. Uncover; cook, turning sausages several times, until lightly browned, about 10 more minutes. Use an instant-read thermometer to confirm internal temperature reaches 160 degrees F; drain. Remove sausages and keep warm.

Return the frying pan to the stove and heat the oil over medium until it shimmers. Add the onion and cook for 2 minutes. Add the bell pepper and cook, stirring occasionally, until tender. Add the garlic and cook for 1 more minute.

Return the sausages to the pan and add the marinara sauce. Cook until sauce bubbles. Use tongs to place a sausage on each bun. Divide the sauce among the buns and sprinkle with the cheese.

Smothered Roast Pork Sandwiches

MAKES 6 SERVINGS

1 (about 2½ pounds)	pork loin roast
	kosher salt and freshly ground black pepper, to taste
2½ cups	beef stock or broth
2 tablespoons	flour
6 slices	whole wheat bread, toasted
½ cup	shredded cheddar cheese

Preheat oven to 425 degrees F.

Sprinkle the pork all over with salt and pepper and place in a roasting pan. Bake for 20 minutes. Reduce oven temperature to 325 degrees F and roast until pork reaches an internal temperature of 145 degrees F, 45–60 minutes. Remove from the oven, tent with aluminum foil, and rest for 10 minutes. Cut the pork into thin slices, removing any fat, and set aside.

In a small bowl, whisk together the stock and flour. Drain the excess fat from the roasting pan and set on the stovetop over medium-high heat. Pour the flour mixture into the pan, whisking frequently, and bring to a simmer. Continue cooking and whisking until gravy is thickened and bubbling, about 5 minutes. Divide the toast slices among six plates and top with sliced pork. Drizzle with gravy, sprinkle with cheese, and serve.

Bacon-Beer Ballpark Brats

MAKES 8 SERVINGS

8 strips	thick-cut bacon
2	large sweet yellow onions, halved and cut into $\frac{1}{4}$-inch slices
2 cups	regular or nonalcoholic beer
1 teaspoon	kosher salt
$\frac{1}{2}$ teaspoon	freshly ground black pepper
8	fresh bratwurst links
8	hoagie or large hot dog buns, split
	stone-ground mustard, for serving

Cook bacon in a large frying pan until brown and crispy. Reserve the drippings and drain bacon on paper towels; crumble and set aside. Add the onions to the pan and cook over medium-low heat, stirring occasionally, until golden brown and caramelized, 30–40 minutes. Transfer the onions to a large, heavy aluminum foil pan.

Preheat a grill to medium. Place the foil pan over indirect heat, stir in the beer, salt, and pepper, and cover pan with aluminum foil. Grill the brats over direct heat, turning often, until browned and cooked through, 15–20 minutes. Transfer brats to the onion mixture, cover again with foil, and simmer for at least 30 minutes and up to 2 hours.

Grill the buns, cut-side down, until lightly toasted, 1–2 minutes. Add crumbled bacon to the onion mixture and stir until combined. To serve, place a bratwurst in each bun and use a slotted spoon to top each bratwurst with some of the onion relish. Serve with stone-ground mustard.

Aloha Pork Sandwiches

MAKES 8 SERVINGS

1 (about 2½ pounds)	**pork loin roast**
2	**red bell peppers, diced**
1	**small yellow onion, diced**
1	**large jalapeño, seeded and diced**
2 cloves	**garlic, minced**
1 cup	**pineapple juice**
½ cup	**soy sauce**
8	**fresh, cored or canned, drained pineapple slices**
8	**sandwich buns, split and toasted**
2 tablespoons	**chopped cilantro, for garnish**

Place the pork roast, bell peppers, onion, jalapeño, garlic, pineapple juice, and soy sauce in a 6-quart slow cooker. Cover and cook until pork is tender, 5–6 hours on high or 7–8 hours on low. Remove the pork and cool for 10 minutes. Shred the meat with 2 forks, removing excess fat, and return to the slow cooker.

Pat the pineapple slices dry with paper towels. Spray a large frying pan with nonstick cooking spray and heat over medium-high heat. Add the pineapple slices, working in batches if necessary, and cook, turning over once halfway during cooking, until lightly browned, 6–8 minutes total.

Arrange the bottom buns on a work surface and top with the pineapple slices. Use a slotted spoon to transfer some of the pork and peppers on each bun. Sprinkle with cilantro and top with the top buns.

Toasty Ham and Havarti Sandwiches

MAKES 4 SERVINGS

8 slices	bread
1/4 cup	real mayonnaise
4 teaspoons	spicy mustard
1/2 pound	thinly sliced Black Forest ham
2	medium tomatoes, cut into 1/4-inch slices, drained
4 slices	Havarti cheese

Preheat oven to 425 degrees F and grease a rimmed baking sheet.

Arrange the bread slices on a work surface and spread evenly with mayonnaise. Arrange 4 of the bread slices, mayonnaise-side down, on prepared baking sheet.

Spread tops of bread slices with mustard and top each with 2 ham slices, 2 tomato slices, and 1 cheese slice. Top with remaining 4 bread slices, mayonnaise-side up. Bake until golden brown, turning over halfway during cooking, about 12 minutes total. Cut on the diagonal and serve.

Ultimate BLTHs

MAKES 4 SERVINGS

8 slices	tomato
¼ teaspoon	kosher salt
¼ teaspoon	freshly ground black pepper
8 slices	sourdough bread, lightly toasted
¼ cup	mayonnaise
4	lettuce leaves
8 slices	thick-cut bacon, crisply cooked and drained
8 thin slices	smoked ham

Arrange tomato slices in a single layer on paper towels. Sprinkle evenly with salt and pepper and let stand for 10 minutes.

Arrange the toast on a work surface and spread each slice with mayonnaise. Divide the tomatoes among 4 toast slices, and top with lettuce, bacon, and ham. Top with the remaining 4 toast slices, mayonnaise-side down. Press gently, cut on the diagonal, and serve.

Parmesan, Ham, and Cheddar Sandwiches

MAKES 4 SERVINGS

8 slices	sourdough bread
4 tablespoons	butter, softened, divided
¼ cup	mayonnaise
4 slices	cheddar cheese
12 slices	smoked ham
¼ cup	grated Parmesan cheese

Arrange bread slices on a work surface and spread with 2 tablespoons softened butter. Flip over and spread 4 bread slices with mayonnaise. On the other 4 slices, top with the cheese slices and then ham. Cover with remaining bread slices, butter-side up.

Melt remaining 2 tablespoons butter in a large heavy frying pan over medium heat. Add 2 sandwiches to the pan and cook until bread is golden, 4–5 minutes.

Flip sandwiches and cook until bread is golden and cheese is melted, 3–4 minutes longer. Transfer sandwiches to a work surface and immediately sprinkle both sides with half of the Parmesan cheese. Repeat process with remaining sandwiches. Cut each on the diagonal and serve hot.

Bacon-Wrapped Cheese Dogs

MAKES 8 SERVINGS

8 strips	regular sliced bacon
1	small onion, thinly sliced
8	hot dogs
4 slices	American cheese
8	hot dog buns, toasted

Preheat oven to 450 degrees F and lightly grease a baking sheet.

In a large frying pan over medium heat, fry bacon until lightly browned but still flexible. Transfer bacon to paper towels to drain, and discard all but 1 tablespoon pan drippings. Return pan to heat and cook the onion, stirring often, until tender and lightly browned, 6–7 minutes; set aside.

Cut each hot dog lengthwise down the middle—almost, but not all the way through. Cut the cheese slices in quarters and fill the pocket of each hot dog with 2 cheese pieces.

Wrap each hot dog with a bacon strip, securing with toothpicks if necessary. Bake until cheese is melted and bacon and hot dog are hot, about 10 minutes. Serve the dogs on the toasted buns topped with the fried onion.

APPETIZERS
&
SNACKS

#33
Honey Soy Pork Bites

MAKES 12 SERVINGS

4 pounds	pork shoulder roast, cut into 1-inch cubes
1	medium onion, coarsely chopped
½ teaspoon	kosher salt
¼ teaspoon	freshly ground black pepper
1 cup	honey
3 tablespoons	soy sauce or tamari
3 cloves	garlic, minced
¼ teaspoon	cayenne pepper
1 teaspoon	sesame seeds

Preheat oven to 350 degrees F.

Put pork and onion in a roasting pan, sprinkle with salt and black pepper, stir, and spread evenly in the pan. Cover with aluminum foil and bake for 1 hour.

In a small bowl, whisk together the honey, soy sauce, garlic, and cayenne pepper. Pour the mixture over the pork, stirring to coat. Continue cooking, uncovered, for 1½ hours, stirring every 20 minutes, until pork bites are deep golden brown.

Remove from the oven, rest for 10 minutes, and transfer pork bites to a serving platter. Sprinkle with sesame seeds and spear with toothpicks for serving.

Chorizo Queso Dip

MAKES 6 SERVINGS

1 pound	ground chorizo
8 ounces	cream cheese, softened
1 can (10 ounces)	diced tomatoes and green chiles, undrained
1 cup	cooked corn (fresh, frozen, or canned)
2 cups	shredded Colby Jack cheese
1	medium tomato, seeded and diced
	chopped chives or minced green onion, for garnish
	tortilla chips, for dipping

In a large frying pan over medium-high heat, cook the chorizo, breaking it up with a spatula, until lightly browned, about 10 minutes. Drain excess grease.

Reduce heat to medium, add the cream cheese to the pan, and cook, stirring constantly, until melted. Add the diced tomatoes and green chiles, corn, and cheese, and cook, stirring occasionally, until mixture just bubbles and cheese is melted.

Remove from the heat and garnish with tomato and chives. Serve with tortilla chips.

Pulled Pork Nachos
MAKES 8 SERVINGS

2 teaspoons	extra-virgin olive oil
½ pound	pulled pork (see page 97), chopped
¼ teaspoon	kosher salt
¼ teaspoon	freshly ground black pepper
10 ounces	large, sturdy restaurant-style tortilla chips
2 cups	shredded Colby Jack cheese
2	small jalapeño peppers, seeded and thinly sliced
½ cup	guacamole
½ cup	pico de gallo or salsa
	optional extras: sour cream, warm queso sauce, chopped red onion, sliced black olives, hot sauce, lime wedges, chopped cilantro

Preheat oven to 375 degrees F and lightly grease a large, rimmed baking sheet.

Brush a heavy frying pan with oil and heat over medium heat until shimmering. Add pork; cook and stir until heated through and slightly crisped, 3–5 minutes. Sprinkle with salt and pepper. Remove from the heat and set aside.

Spread chips on the prepared sheet in a single layer, slightly overlapping but not stacked. Sprinkle with half of the cheese and bake until cheese just starts to melt, 3–4 minutes.

Sprinkle the pulled pork evenly on the chips, and top with the jalapeño slices. Sprinkle evenly with the remaining cheese. Bake until cheese is melted, 5–7 minutes. Serve nachos hot with guacamole and pico de gallo on the side, plus optional toppings.

Mozzarella-Stuffed Sausage Meatballs

MAKES 8 SERVINGS

1	egg, lightly beaten
1/3 cup	Italian seasoned breadcrumbs
1/4 cup	grated Parmesan cheese
1/4 cup	milk
1/4 cup	finely chopped onion
1/4 teaspoon	fine sea salt
1/4 teaspoon	freshly ground black pepper
1 1/4 pounds	bulk Italian sausage
20	mini fresh mozzarella cheese balls
1 cup	marinara sauce

Preheat oven to 350 degrees F and lightly grease a large, rimmed baking sheet.

In a large bowl, combine the egg, breadcrumbs, Parmesan cheese, milk, onion, salt, and pepper. Add sausage to the breadcrumb mixture and mix well.

Shape into 20 meatballs, pressing 1 ball of cheese in the center of each meatball, and covering it completely with the meat mixture.

Arrange meatballs on prepared baking sheet. Bake until meatballs are lightly browned and cooked through (160 degrees F), 20–25 minutes. Cool on the pan for 5 minutes and drain on paper towels.

While the meatballs are baking, heat the marinara sauce in a saucepan over medium heat until it just starts to simmer. Remove from the heat and transfer to a heatproof bowl. Spear the meatballs on toothpicks and serve with the marinara sauce for dipping.

#37
Loaded Potato Skins

MAKES 12 SERVINGS

6 (about 3 pounds)	medium russet potatoes
4 tablespoons	butter, melted
	kosher salt and freshly ground black pepper, to taste
12 strips	bacon, cooked and crumbled
1 cup	shredded cheddar cheese
½ cup	sour cream
2	green onions, thinly sliced

Preheat oven to 400 degrees F.

Arrange potatoes on the middle rack and bake, turning once halfway during cooking, until tender, about 1 hour.

Cool for 10 minutes. Cut potatoes in half horizontally and use a spoon to carefully scoop out the insides, leaving a "shell" about ¼ inch thick. (Reserve scooped-out potatoes for another use.) Cut each shell in half lengthwise.

Increase the oven temperature to 450 degrees F. Brush potatoes with melted butter and sprinkle with salt and pepper. Arrange on a baking sheet and cook for 10 minutes; turn over and continue baking for 8–10 minutes or until potato skins are golden brown and crispy. Sprinkle with bacon and cheese and return to the oven. Cook for 2–3 more minutes, or until cheese is melted. Top with sour cream and green onions just before serving.

BBQ Pork Burnt Ends
MAKES 12 SERVINGS

½ cup	dark brown sugar, packed
¼ cup	apple cider vinegar
2 tablespoons	Worcestershire sauce
2 tablespoons	Dijon mustard
2 teaspoons	smoked or regular paprika
2 teaspoons	garlic powder
2 teaspoons	onion powder
½ teaspoon	freshly ground black pepper
¼ teaspoon	fine sea salt
2 pounds	boneless pork shoulder, cut into 1¼-inch cubes
6 strips	thick-cut bacon, cooked and crumbled
½ cup	honey barbecue sauce

Preheat oven to 300 degrees F and grease a large baking dish.

In a large bowl, whisk together the brown sugar, vinegar, Worcestershire sauce, mustard, paprika, garlic powder, onion powder, pepper, and salt. Add the pork cubes and bacon and stir to coat evenly. Transfer to the prepared baking dish and cover with aluminum foil.

Bake for 2 hours. Remove foil, drizzle with barbecue sauce, and stir to combine. Return to the oven and bake uncovered, stirring every 20 minutes, until the sauce thickens and pork is browned, about 1 hour. Cool for 10 minutes and transfer the pork to a serving platter. Spear the cubes with toothpicks and serve warm.

Ham and Cheese Spud Bites

MAKES ABOUT 72 PIECES

3½ cups	cornflakes, crushed
2 cups	leftover mashed potatoes
1 pound	cooked ham, finely chopped
1 cup	shredded Swiss cheese
½ cup	mayonnaise
¼ cup	finely chopped onion
1	egg, beaten
1 teaspoon	prepared yellow mustard
½ teaspoon	fine sea salt
¼ teaspoon	freshly ground black pepper

Preheat oven to 350 degrees F and grease a large, rimmed baking sheet.

Pour the crushed cornflakes in a large shallow bowl.

In a large bowl, combine the potatoes, ham, cheese, mayonnaise, onion, egg, mustard, salt, and pepper and stir until blended. Shape mixture into 1-inch balls and roll in cornflakes, pressing to coat evenly. Arrange on the prepared baking sheet, about 1 inch apart, and bake until lightly browned, 20–25 minutes. Serve warm.

Bacon-Wrapped Bratwurst Bites

MAKES 16 PIECES

4 (about 14 ounces)	fresh bratwurst links
1 can or bottle (12 ounces)	regular or nonalcoholic beer
6 tablespoons	light brown sugar, packed
$\frac{1}{2}$ teaspoon	freshly ground black pepper
$\frac{1}{4}$ teaspoon	cayenne pepper
8 strips	bacon, cut in half

Preheat oven to 350 degrees F. Line a rimmed baking sheet with aluminum foil, place a wire rack on top, and set aside.

Arrange the bratwurst in a medium frying pan and pour the beer around them. Turn the heat to medium-high and bring to a boil. Reduce heat to low, cover, and simmer for 15 minutes. Remove the bratwurst from the beer and drain on paper towels. Discard the beer.

In a medium bowl, combine the brown sugar, black pepper, and cayenne; set aside. Cut each bratwurst into 4 pieces, wrap each piece with half strip of bacon, and secure with a toothpick. Toss the bacon-wrapped bratwurst in the sugar mixture to coat, and arrange on the wire rack on baking sheet. Bake, turning once halfway through baking, until the bacon is brown and crisp, 25–30 minutes.

Teriyaki Pork Meatballs

MAKES 18 PIECES

¼ cup	reduced-sodium soy sauce
3 tablespoons	dark brown sugar, packed
1 tablespoon	rice vinegar
4 cloves	garlic, minced, divided
½ teaspoon	ground ginger
1½ teaspoons	cornstarch
1 pound	lean ground pork
2 tablespoons	minced onion
1	green onion, minced
1	egg
½ cup	panko crumbs
	sesame seeds, for garnish

Preheat oven to 350 degrees F.

In a small bowl, whisk together the soy sauce, brown sugar, vinegar, half of the minced garlic, ginger, and cornstarch; set aside.

In a large bowl, combine the pork, onion, green onion, egg, and panko crumbs, and mix just until combined. Divide and roll the mixture into 18 meatballs, and arrange in a large cast-iron or oven-safe frying pan.

Cook the meatballs over medium-high heat, turning occasionally, until lightly browned on all sides, about 6 minutes. Move the frying pan to the oven and bake until meatballs are lightly browned and cooked through (160 degrees F), 15–20 minutes.

Return the frying pan to the stove over medium-low heat and add the remaining half of the minced garlic. Cook until fragrant, add the sauce, and cook, stirring frequently, until sauce thickens and coats the meatballs. Cool the meatballs for 5 minutes, transfer to a serving platter, and spear with toothpicks. Sprinkle with sesame seeds and serve warm.

#42

Bacon-Wrapped Smokies

MAKES 30–36 PIECES

14 ounces	pork cocktail wieners
1 pound	regular sliced bacon, cut into thirds
$\frac{1}{3}$ cup	honey barbecue sauce or sauce of your choice

Preheat oven to 325 degrees F. Line a large baking sheet with parchment paper.

Wrap each cocktail wiener with a piece of bacon and arrange on the baking sheet seam-side down. Bake, turning several times, until the bacon is crispy and brown, about 40 minutes.

Remove from the oven and turn on the broiler. Brush the bacon-wrapped smokies all over with barbecue sauce. Return to the oven and broil until sauce bubbles, about 1 minute. Cool pan on a wire rack for 5 minutes. Skewer sausages with toothpicks, arrange on a platter, and serve.

Sausage-Stuffed Mushrooms

MAKES 12 PIECES

12	large fresh mushrooms
2 tablespoons	butter
2 tablespoons	chopped sweet onion (such as Vidalia)
1 tablespoon	lemon juice
1 tablespoon	chopped fresh basil
	kosher salt and freshly grated black pepper, to taste
4 ounces	bulk Italian sausage
1 tablespoon	chopped fresh parsley
2 tablespoons	dry breadcrumbs
2 tablespoons	grated Parmesan cheese
	chopped chives, for garnish

Preheat oven to 400 degrees F and lightly grease a large, rimmed baking sheet.

Remove stems from mushrooms and finely chop; set aside. Arrange mushroom caps, stem-side up, on prepared baking sheet and set aside.

In a frying pan, heat the butter over medium-high heat and cook the onion and mushroom stems until tender, about 5 minutes. Add lemon juice, basil, salt, and pepper and cook until most of the juices have evaporated. Cool slightly.

In a small bowl, combine the sausage, parsley, and onion mixture until blended. Divide the mixture evenly among the mushroom caps, mounding slightly to fill.

In a small dish, whisk together breadcrumbs and Parmesan cheese until blended, and sprinkle the mixture over the filling in the mushroom caps. Bake until tops start to brown and internal temperature of sausage mixture measures 160 degrees F on an instant-read thermometer, about 20 minutes. Cool on pan for 5 minutes, and sprinkle with chopped chives before serving.

#44
Ham–Dill Pickle Dip
MAKES 8 SERVINGS

8 ounces	cream cheese, softened
1 cup	sour cream
3 tablespoons	ranch dressing seasoning mix
1 cup	whole dill pickles, drained and cut into $\frac{1}{4}$-inch dice
1 cup	chopped deli sliced ham
1	green onion, finely minced assorted crackers, chips, and veggies

In a medium bowl, mix the cream cheese, sour cream, and ranch dressing mix until smooth.

Add the diced pickles, chopped ham, and green onion, and stir until well combined. Serve with crackers, chips, or veggies for dipping.

Crunchy Bacon Breadsticks

MAKES 12 SERVINGS

1/2 cup	grated Parmesan cheese
1 teaspoon	garlic powder
1/4 teaspoon	freshly ground black pepper
12 (6-inch)	sesame seed breadsticks
12 strips	regular sliced bacon

Preheat oven to 350 degrees F and line a baking sheet with parchment paper.

Combine the Parmesan cheese, garlic powder, and pepper in a shallow dish that will fit the breadsticks (a pie dish works well) and set aside.

Wrap each breadstick with a slice of bacon, spiraling it around and pressing gently to stick. Arrange the breadsticks on the prepared baking sheet.

Bake, turning breadsticks over once halfway through cooking, until bacon is browned, 15–20 minutes. Remove from the oven and immediately roll each breadstick in the cheese mixture, returning to the baking sheet to cool after coating in the cheese. Cool for 5 minutes before serving.

Cheesy Sausage Balls

MAKES 12 SERVINGS

1 pound	spicy pork sausage
8 ounces	cream cheese, softened
2 cups	biscuit mix, such as Bisquick
1 cup	shredded sharp cheddar cheese
	ranch dressing, for dipping

Line 2 large baking sheets with parchment paper.

In a large bowl, mix together the sausage and cream cheese. Add the biscuit mix and stir until combined. Add the cheese and stir until just incorporated.

Use a spoon to form the mixture into 1-inch balls. Roll and arrange on the prepared baking sheets. Refrigerate for 15 minutes. While sausage balls are chilling, preheat oven to 350 degrees F.

Remove baking sheets from refrigerator and bake until sausage balls are lightly browned, about 25 minutes. Serve with ranch dressing.

Pork Lettuce Wraps

MAKES 8 SERVINGS

2 teaspoons	extra-virgin olive oil
1 tablespoon	finely chopped fresh peeled ginger
2 cloves	garlic, minced
1 pound	lean ground pork
1/4 cup	hoisin sauce
2 teaspoons	sriracha sauce
1 head (8 leaves)	butter lettuce, separated
1	medium carrot, cut into 1/4-inch dice
1/4 cup	fresh bean sprouts
1	green onion, finely chopped tamari or reduced-sodium soy sauce, for dipping

In a large frying pan over medium heat, heat the oil until it shimmers. Add ginger and garlic and cook until fragrant, 2 minutes. Add pork and cook, breaking up with a spatula, until cooked through and no longer pink, 6–7 minutes. Add hoisin sauce and sriracha sauce, and cook, stirring occasionally, until hot, about 2 minutes.

Spoon pork mixture into lettuce leaves and sprinkle with carrot, bean sprouts, and green onion. Roll up and serve with tamari for dipping.

SIDES
&
SALADS

#48
Southern Black-Eyed Peas
MAKES 10 SERVINGS

1 pound	dried black-eyed peas
6 cups	chicken stock
1	medium sweet yellow onion, chopped
2 cloves	garlic, minced
1 teaspoon	kosher salt
$\frac{1}{2}$ teaspoon	freshly ground black pepper
$\frac{1}{4}$ teaspoon	cayenne pepper
1	large ham hock or 2 cups cooked, cubed ham

Rinse the dried peas in a strainer. Transfer to a large Dutch oven.

Add the chicken stock, onion, garlic, salt, black pepper, cayenne, and ham. Bring to a boil over medium-high heat. Cover, reduce heat, and simmer until peas are tender, about 1½ hours. If using ham hock, remove from pot and cool. Chop meat and return it to the pot. Stir and serve.

#49

Deviled Eggs with Bacon

MAKES 16 EGGS

8	hard-boiled eggs, peeled
1/3 cup	mayonnaise
1 teaspoon	prepared yellow mustard
1/4 teaspoon	curry powder
1/4 teaspoon	fine sea salt
1/8 teaspoon	freshly ground black pepper
4 slices	bacon, cooked and crumbled

Cut each egg in half lengthwise; gently scoop out yolks and place in a bowl. Mash yolks with a fork, then stir in mayonnaise, mustard, and curry powder until well blended. Add salt and pepper.

Spoon or pipe about 1 tablespoon yolk mixture into the hollow of each egg half. Serve immediately or cover and chill up to 4 hours, garnishing with crumbled bacon just before serving.

Pork Lovers' Maple Baked Beans

MAKES 8–10 SERVINGS

2 cups	dried navy beans
1½ cups	water, plus extra for cooking beans
½ cup	regular or nonalcoholic beer
½ cup	maple syrup
1 teaspoon	dry mustard
1 teaspoon	kosher salt
6 strips	bacon, cooked and crumbled
1	onion, chopped
1	smoked ham hock

Preheat oven to 325 degrees F.

Place the beans in a large pot, add enough water to cover beans by 2 inches, and bring to a boil over high heat. Boil for 30 minutes. Drain beans and discard cooking liquid.

In a medium bowl, combine water, beer, maple syrup, mustard, and salt. Place the bacon in the bottom of a Dutch oven and spoon half of the beans and half of the onion evenly over top. Add the ham hock and remaining beans and onion. Pour the maple syrup mixture over the beans and cover with a lid. Bake for 3 hours, or until beans are tender and the meat from the ham hock pulls away from the bone. (If beans become dry during cooking, add ¼ cup more water.)

Remove pot from oven and transfer the ham hock to a cutting board to cool. Chop the meat and stir into the beans.

#51

Million-Dollar Potatoes

MAKES 8 SERVINGS

10	medium Yukon Gold potatoes, peeled and halved
8 strips	thick-sliced bacon
2 cups	shredded sharp cheddar cheese, divided
1 cup	half-and-half
$\frac{1}{2}$ cup	sour cream
$\frac{1}{3}$ cup	finely chopped green onions, divided
1 teaspoon	fine sea salt
$\frac{1}{2}$ teaspoon	freshly ground black pepper

Preheat oven to 350 degrees F and grease a 9 x 13-inch baking dish.

Place potatoes in a large pot and cover with salted water; bring to a boil over high heat. Reduce heat to medium-low and simmer until tender, about 20 minutes. Drain and return potatoes to the pot to dry. While the potatoes are cooking, fry the bacon in a large frying pan over medium-high heat, turning once, until brown and crispy, about 10 minutes. Drain bacon on paper towels, crumble, and set aside.

Add 1$\frac{1}{2}$ cups cheese, half-and-half, sour cream, half of the green onions, half of the crumbled bacon, salt, and black pepper to the pot with potatoes and mash with a potato masher until creamy.

Spread mixture into the prepared baking dish. Bake in the preheated oven for 25 minutes. Sprinkle with remaining $\frac{1}{2}$ cup cheese, green onions, and bacon. Return to the oven and continue cooking until cheese is melted, about 5 minutes.

Easy Sausage Herb Stuffing
MAKES 6 SERVINGS

1 pound	mild bulk Italian sausage
1	medium yellow onion, diced
3 stalks	celery, diced
2 teaspoons	minced fresh sage
2 teaspoons	minced fresh thyme
2¼ cups	chicken stock or broth
3 tablespoons	butter
1 bag (12 ounces)	herb-seasoned cubed stuffing mix

Preheat oven to 350 degrees F. Lightly grease a 9 x 13-inch baking dish.

In a large frying pan over medium heat, cook the sausage, breaking up with a spatula, for 5 minutes. Add the onion, celery, sage, and thyme. Stir to combine. Continue cooking until the sausage is lightly browned and the vegetables are tender, about 10 minutes.

Add the chicken stock and butter. Continue cooking over medium heat until the stock simmers and butter is melted. Remove from the heat, add the stuffing mix, and use a fork to toss the bread cubes with the liquid. Transfer to prepared baking dish. Cover with aluminum foil and bake for 30 minutes. Remove foil and continue baking until lightly browned and heated through, about 10 minutes.

Skillet Bacon Cornbread

MAKES 8 SERVINGS

1½ cups	cornmeal
½ cup	flour
2 teaspoons	baking powder
1 teaspoon	sugar
1 teaspoon	fine sea salt
¼ teaspoon	baking soda
¼ cup	vegetable oil
1½ cups	buttermilk
2	eggs, beaten
6 strips	bacon

Preheat oven to 425 degrees F.

In a bowl, whisk together the cornmeal, flour, baking powder, sugar, salt, and baking soda. Make a well in the dry ingredients and add oil, buttermilk, and eggs; stir until just combined.

In a medium cast-iron frying pan with an oven-safe handle, cook the bacon over medium heat until crispy. Transfer the bacon to paper towels and crumble. Pour out all but 1 tablespoon bacon drippings from the frying pan and heat over medium. Add the crumbled bacon to the batter and stir until just combined. Pour mixture in the hot frying pan and bake for 20–25 minutes or until golden brown and center springs back when lightly pressed. Cool and cut into wedges.

Slow-Cooked Green Beans with Ham

MAKES 10 SERVINGS

2 pounds	fresh green beans, strings removed and ends trimmed
1	large smoked ham hock
6 cups	chicken stock or broth
2 cloves	garlic, minced
½ cup	diced sweet yellow onion
2 teaspoons	kosher salt
½ teaspoon	freshly ground black pepper
½ teaspoon	red pepper flakes
1 teaspoon	balsamic vinegar
	chopped flat-leaf parsley, for garnish

In a 5-quart slow cooker, combine the green beans, ham hock, chicken stock, garlic, onion, salt, black pepper, red pepper flakes, and vinegar. Stir to combine and cook on high for 5–6 hours or low for 8 hours, until the ham is tender and falls off the bone.

Transfer the ham hock to a cutting board to cool. Chop the meat and stir into the beans. Serve garnished with parsley.

Bacon-Fried Cabbage

MAKES 4 SERVINGS

½	**large head green cabbage**
8 strips	**thick-sliced bacon**
1 tablespoon	**unsalted butter**
2 cloves	**garlic, minced**
½ teaspoon	**kosher salt**
¼ teaspoon	**freshly ground black pepper**

Cut the cabbage into 1-inch slices, then cut each slice into 1-inch pieces; set aside. Chop the bacon into ½-inch pieces. In a large frying pan over medium heat, cook the bacon, stirring occasionally, until it starts to brown, about 8 minutes. Remove the bacon from the pan with a slotted spoon and drain it on paper towels; set aside.

Pour out the liquid fat from the pan, leaving the bacon drippings in the pan. Return to the stove, add the butter to the pan, and heat over medium-high heat until the butter bubbles. Add the cabbage and bacon. Cook, stirring often and scraping the bits up from the pan. After 3 minutes, add the garlic to the pan and continue cooking, stirring frequently, until cabbage is crisp-tender, 3–5 more minutes. Season with salt and pepper. Remove from the heat and serve at once.

Dirty Rice
MAKES 6 SERVINGS

1 pound	mild bulk pork sausage
1	medium yellow onion, diced
1	medium green bell pepper, seeded and diced
3 stalks	celery, chopped
3 cloves	garlic, minced
2 teaspoons	Cajun seasoning
1½ cups	uncooked long-grain white rice
4 cups	chicken stock or broth
2 sprigs	thyme
	kosher salt and freshly ground black pepper, to taste
	chopped chives or green onions, for garnish

In a medium heavy-bottom pot over medium-high heat, cook the sausage, breaking up with a spatula, until lightly browned, about 8 minutes. Drain and discard excess grease, then return the pot to the stove.

Add the onion, bell pepper, and celery. Cook, stirring frequently, until vegetables are tender, about 8 minutes. Add the garlic and cook for 1 more minute. Sprinkle with the Cajun seasoning and stir.

Add rice, chicken stock, and thyme, and continue cooking until mixture comes to a rolling boil. Reduce heat to medium-low, cover, and simmer until rice is tender, about 20 minutes. Add salt and pepper. Garnish with chives.

Bacon and Maple Carrots

MAKES 8 SERVINGS

6 (about 1½ pounds)	large carrots
12 ounces	regular or thick-cut smoked bacon
2 tablespoons	pure maple syrup
½ teaspoon	kosher salt
½ teaspoon	freshly ground black pepper
1 teaspoon	chopped fresh oregano, for garnish

Peel and cut the carrots into ½-inch-thick sticks, varying length from 1½ to 3 inches, and set aside. Cut the bacon strips into 1-inch squares.

In a large frying pan over medium heat, cook the bacon, stirring occasionally, until lightly browned and almost fully cooked. Drain bacon on paper towels and pour out all but 1 tablespoon of the pan drippings.

Return the frying pan to the stove, add the carrots, and cook over medium-high heat, stirring frequently, for 3 minutes. Stir in the maple syrup and continue cooking, stirring occasionally, until carrots are tender, 6–8 minutes. Add the bacon pieces and cook for 2 more minutes. Sprinkle with salt and pepper and stir. Serve garnished with fresh oregano.

Autumn Salad with Pork Tenderloin

MAKES 8 SERVINGS

1 (1-pound)	pork tenderloin, patted dry
1 tablespoon	extra-virgin olive oil
1 teaspoon	kosher salt
1/2 teaspoon	freshly ground black pepper
8 cups	chopped romaine lettuce
2 cups	spring mix lettuce
2	small Granny Smith apples, sliced thin
1 cup	dried cherries
1/2 cup	shelled, roasted pistachio nuts
6 strips	bacon, cooked and crumbled
3 ounces	Gorgonzola cheese, crumbled creamy poppy-seed dressing, or your favorite salad dressing, for drizzling

Preheat oven to 425 degrees F with racks in the upper third position. Line a rimmed baking sheet with aluminum foil and set a wire baking rack inside.

Brush pork all over with oil and sprinkle with salt and pepper. Place on prepared rack and bake, turning over once during cooking, until center of pork registers 145 degrees F using an instant-read thermometer, about 30 minutes. Let pork rest 10 minutes before cutting into 16 thin slices.

In a large bowl, toss the lettuces, apples, cherries, pistachios, bacon, and Gorgonzola. Divide among eight salad plates and top each with 2 warm pork slices. Drizzle with dressing or serve it on the side.

Pork Cobb Salad

MAKES 8 SERVINGS

1¼ cups	barbecue sauce
½ teaspoon	garlic powder
¼ teaspoon	paprika
1 (1-pound)	pork tenderloin
6 cups	chopped romaine lettuce
6 cups	chopped iceberg lettuce
3	medium tomatoes, chopped and drained
2	avocados, peeled and chopped
1	medium red or orange bell pepper, chopped
6 strips	bacon, cooked and crumbled
3	hard-boiled eggs, peeled and chopped
1½ cups	shredded cheddar cheese
½ cup	ranch or blue cheese salad dressing, for drizzling

In a 5-quart slow cooker, combine the barbecue sauce, garlic powder, and paprika. Add the pork and use tongs to coat with the sauce mixture. Cook, covered, on low temperature until pork is tender, 4–5 hours. Remove pork from slow cooker, cool for 10 minutes, and chop into bite-size pieces. In a medium bowl, toss pork with 1 cup of liquid from the slow cooker. Cool to room temperature and set aside.

Arrange lettuces on a large serving platter. Arrange the tomatoes, avocados, bell pepper, bacon, eggs, cheese, and pork in rows over the lettuces. Drizzle with dressing or serve on the side.

Warm Bacon Potato Salad

MAKES 10 SERVINGS

1 pound	smoked sliced bacon, chopped in $\frac{1}{2}$-inch pieces
3 pounds	potatoes, peeled and cut into $\frac{1}{4}$-inch bite-size slices
1	sweet yellow onion, such as Vidalia, chopped
3 tablespoons	flour
$\frac{3}{4}$ cup	water
1 tablespoon	sugar
1 tablespoon	brown sugar, packed
$\frac{1}{3}$ cup	apple cider vinegar
	kosher salt and freshly ground black pepper, to taste
	chopped fresh chives, for garnish

Cook the bacon in a large frying pan over medium heat until golden brown, stirring occasionally. Drain on paper towels and set aside. Remove the frying pan from the heat and drain all but 3 tablespoons bacon drippings; reserve.

Put the potatoes in a large pot and cover with cold water. Cook until water comes to a boil and potatoes are tender, about 20 minutes.

While potatoes are cooking, heat the reserved bacon drippings in the frying pan over medium heat. Add the onion and cook, stirring occasionally, until tender and just starting to brown, about 10 minutes. Sprinkle with the flour and cook, stirring to blend, for 1 minute. Add the water, sugars, and vinegar, and whisk to blend. Continue cooking and whisking until mixture thickens.

When potatoes are tender, drain in a colander, shake, and let sit for a few minutes to dry. Add the potatoes to the frying pan dressing. Set aside about 2 tablespoons crumbled bacon for garnish, and add the rest to the pan, stirring to combine. Transfer to a serving dish and garnish with chopped chives and reserved bacon.

Southwest Taco Salad

MAKES 8 SERVINGS

1 pound	ground pork
1 packet (1 ounce)	taco seasoning mix
1 can (15 ounces)	black beans, drained and rinsed
3/4 cup	water
10 cups	torn romaine and/or iceberg lettuce
2	medium tomatoes, chopped
3/4 cup	cooked corn, room temperature
1/4 cup	chopped red onion
2 cups	shredded cheddar cheese
1/2 cup	Western salad dressing
	tortilla chips, broken in pieces
	salsa, sour cream, and guacamole, for serving

In a large frying pan, cook pork over medium heat, breaking up with a spatula, until lightly browned, about 10 minutes. Drain and discard excess grease. Add the taco seasoning, beans, and water and bring to a boil, stirring occasionally. Reduce heat and simmer, uncovered, for 5 minutes, stirring occasionally. Remove from the heat and cool for 15 minutes.

In a large bowl, combine the lettuce, tomatoes, corn, onion, and cheese. Stir in pork mixture. Drizzle with salad dressing and toss to coat. Sprinkle with chips. Serve immediately with salsa, sour cream, and guacamole on the side.

#62
Hog-Wild Wedge Salad
MAKES 6 SERVINGS

1 head	iceberg lettuce
1 cup	chopped leftover pulled pork*
1	large tomato, finely chopped and drained
2 ounces	blue cheese, crumbled
6 strips	thick-cut bacon, crisply cooked and crumbled
	kosher salt and freshly ground black pepper, to taste
2/3 cup	buttermilk ranch dressing

Trim the bottom of the lettuce and cut it into six wedges. Cut each wedge into 3 pieces and arrange on each of six chilled salad plates.

Top with the pulled pork, tomato, crumbled blue cheese, and bacon. Sprinkle with salt and pepper. Drizzle with salad dressing and serve.

*See page 97 for Perfect Pulled Pork recipe.

Grandma's Ham Salad
MAKES 6 SERVINGS

¾ cup	mayonnaise
1 tablespoon	dill or sweet pickle relish, undrained
2 teaspoons	Dijon mustard
½ teaspoon	fine sea salt
¼ teaspoon	freshly ground black pepper
2 cups	finely chopped cooked ham
1 stalk	celery, chopped
¼ cup	finely chopped sweet onion, such as Vidalia
2	hard-boiled eggs, peeled and chopped
2 teaspoons	chopped fresh parsley, for garnish

In a large bowl, whisk together the mayonnaise, pickle relish, mustard, salt, and pepper. Add the ham, celery, onion, and eggs, and stir the mixture gently to combine. Cover and chill for 1 hour to blend flavors. Garnish with parsley before serving.

MAIN
COURSES

Sausage Stroganoff

MAKES 4 SERVINGS

8 ounces	uncooked wide egg noodles
2 teaspoons	extra-virgin olive oil
4	fully cooked pork sausage links, cut into ¼-inch-thick diagonal slices
1	medium onion, chopped
2 cloves	garlic, minced
½ pound	button mushrooms, cleaned and sliced
¼ cup	flour
¼ teaspoon	kosher salt
½ teaspoon	paprika
1½ cups	beef stock or broth
1 cup	sour cream
	kosher salt and freshly ground black pepper, to taste
	chopped flat-leaf parsley, for garnish

Cook noodles according to package directions and keep warm.

Heat the oil in a large frying pan over medium heat and add the sausage. Cook for 2 minutes and add the onion, garlic, and mushrooms. Cook, stirring often, until mushrooms are lightly browned and onion is tender, about 7 minutes.

In small bowl, whisk together flour, salt, and paprika. Add stock and whisk until combined. Add to the sausage mixture and cook until thickened and bubbling, 3–4 minutes. Remove from the heat, add the sour cream, and stir until just combined. Season to taste with salt and pepper. Serve over hot noodles and garnish with parsley.

Crispy Breaded Pork Chops
MAKES 4 SERVINGS

1	**egg**
1 teaspoon	**water**
½ cup	**panko crumbs**
2 tablespoons	**grated Parmesan cheese**
½ teaspoon	**garlic powder**
¼ teaspoon	**paprika**
¼ teaspoon	**fine sea salt**
¼ teaspoon	**freshly ground black pepper**
¼ cup	**flour**
4 (1-inch-thick)	**boneless pork chops**
2 tablespoons	**vegetable oil**

Preheat oven to 425 degrees F. Line a rimmed baking sheet with parchment paper.

In a shallow bowl, whisk the egg and water together until well beaten. In another shallow bowl, combine panko crumbs, Parmesan cheese, garlic powder, paprika, salt, and pepper; set aside.

Put the flour in a gallon ziplock bag. Add the pork chops and shake to coat. Dip each pork chop in the egg mixture, coating all sides. Quickly dip each pork chop in the panko crumb mixture, coating all sides.

Heat oil in a large frying pan over medium-high heat until it shimmers. Cook pork chops, turning once, until brown on both sides, about 4 minutes total. Transfer to prepared baking sheet and bake until an instant-read thermometer reads 145 degrees F, 10–12 minutes. Cool for 5 minutes and serve.

Fried Onion–Pork Chop Bake
MAKES 6 SERVINGS

³/₄ cup	flour
1 teaspoon	fine sea salt
½ teaspoon	freshly ground black pepper
¼ teaspoon	paprika
6 (³/₄–1 inch thick)	boneless pork chops
2 tablespoons	vegetable oil
1 can (10 ³/₄ ounces)	condensed cream of mushroom soup
²/₃ cup	chicken broth or stock
1 cup	sour cream
1 can (2 ⁷/₈ ounces)	french-fried onions, divided

Preheat oven to 350 degrees F.

In a shallow bowl, combine the flour, salt, pepper, and paprika. Dredge the pork chops in the mixture. Heat the oil in a large frying pan over medium heat until it shimmers. Cook pork chops until browned, about 5 minutes per side.

Arrange pork chops in a single layer in a lightly greased 9 x 13-inch baking dish. In a medium bowl, combine cream of mushroom soup, chicken broth, and sour cream; pour over chops. Sprinkle with half of the french-fried onions. Cover and bake until bubbling and pork chops reach an internal temperature of 145 degrees F, 45–50 minutes. Top chops with the remaining half of the french-fried onions and return to the oven, uncovered, for 10 minutes.

#67

Slow-Cooker Red Beans and Rice

MAKES 8 SERVINGS

3 cans (15 ounces each)	**red kidney beans**
½ pound	**smoked andouille sausage, cut into ¼-inch slices**
2 stalks	**celery, chopped**
1	**medium red bell pepper, seeded and chopped**
1	**medium yellow onion, chopped**
2 cloves	**garlic, minced**
1 tablespoon	**Worcestershire sauce**
½ teaspoon	**kosher salt**
¼ teaspoon	**chili powder**
4 cups	**uncooked long-grain rice**
	chopped flat-leaf parsley, for garnish

In a 6-quart slow cooker, combine the beans, sausage, celery, bell pepper, onion, garlic, Worcestershire sauce, salt, and chili powder, and stir to combine. Put the lid on and cook on high for 4 hours or low for 6–8 hours.

About 30 minutes before serving time, cook rice according to package directions. Spoon red beans over top of the cooked rice. Top with parsley and serve.

Divine Bacon Pork Chops

MAKES 4 SERVINGS

4 (1-inch-thick)	**boneless pork chops**
1/2 teaspoon	**kosher salt**
1/4 teaspoon	**freshly ground black pepper**
8 strips	**smoked bacon, chopped**
1 tablespoon	**flour**
1/2 cup	**chicken stock or broth**
3/4 cup	**heavy cream**
	chopped flat-leaf parsley, for garnish

Remove the pork chops from the refrigerator and set on the counter for 30 minutes to take the chill off. Season with salt and pepper and set aside.

In a large frying pan over medium heat, cook the bacon, stirring occasionally, until brown and crispy, 8–10 minutes. Drain on paper towels and set aside. Pour out all but 2 tablespoons of the pan drippings. Add the pork chops to the frying pan, increase the heat to medium-high, and brown both sides, 6–7 minutes. Drain on paper towels, keeping drippings in the frying pan.

Return the frying pan to the stove and reduce heat to medium. Sprinkle the flour in the drippings and cook, stirring, for 1 minute. Add the chicken stock and whisk to blend. Cook until mixture bubbles and thickens, 3–4 minutes. Add the cream and cook for 2 more minutes. Transfer the pork chops to the frying pan and sprinkle with the bacon. Cook until pork chops measure an internal temperature of 145 degrees F and sauce is hot and bubbling. Serve chops topped with some of the sauce and a sprinkle of parsley.

Easy Cola Pork

MAKES 10 SERVINGS

1 tablespoon	dark brown sugar, packed
1 tablespoon	chili powder
1 teaspoon	cumin
1 teaspoon	garlic powder
1 teaspoon	onion powder
1 teaspoon	kosher salt
1 teaspoon	freshly ground black pepper
1 (about 4 pounds)	pork shoulder roast, trimmed of excess fat
2 tablespoons	vegetable oil
1 can (12 ounces or 1½ cups)	cola
	barbecue sauce, for serving

Preheat oven to 300 degrees F.

In a small bowl, whisk together the brown sugar, chili powder, cumin, garlic powder, onion powder, salt, and pepper. Rub mixture evenly all over the pork. Cover and refrigerate for 4 hours, or overnight.

In a Dutch oven, heat the oil over medium-high heat until it shimmers. Sear the roast, turning several times with tongs, until browned all over, 10–12 minutes.

Remove pan from heat and slowly pour the cola around the pork. Cover with lid and bake for 3 hours, checking occasionally. Remove lid and continue cooking until pork is fork-tender, 1–1½ more hours. Remove from oven, cover, and rest for 15 minutes. Use two forks to shred meat, discarding any fat, and serve with barbecue sauce.

Best Easy Spareribs
MAKES 6 SERVINGS

2 racks	pork spareribs, trimmed of excess fat and membrane
1/3 cup	Liquid Smoke flavoring
1 teaspoon	garlic powder
1 1/2 teaspoons	kosher salt
1 teaspoon	freshly ground black pepper
1/2 cup	water
2 cups	barbecue sauce, plus extra for serving
	peanut or canola oil, for brushing grill

Preheat oven to 300 degrees F and move the oven rack to the center of the oven.

Arrange the ribs in a roasting pan and brush with the Liquid Smoke flavoring on both sides. Sprinkle both sides with the garlic powder, salt, and pepper.

Pour the water in a corner of the pan, being careful not to pour the water over the ribs. Cover the pan tightly with aluminum foil. Bake ribs for 2 1/2 hours. About 30 minutes before the ribs are done, preheat a grill to medium-high heat.

Remove the pan from the oven and cool on a rack for 10 minutes before removing foil. Transfer the ribs to a large pan or platter and brush all over with barbecue sauce.

Brush the grill grate with peanut oil to prevent sticking. Arrange the rib racks on the grill and cook until grill marks appear and barbecue sauce gets sticky, about 6 minutes per side. Transfer the ribs from the grill to a pan or platter and tent with foil. Allow to rest for 10 minutes. Use a sharp knife to cut between the ribs. Serve with additional barbecue sauce.

Pork Tenders with Honey Mustard

MAKES 6 SERVINGS

1 tablespoon	vegetable oil
3 tablespoons	honey
2 tablespoons	Dijon mustard
2 tablespoons	mayonnaise
1½ pounds	lean pork tenderloin, fat trimmed
¾ cup	dry breadcrumbs
½ teaspoon	paprika
½ teaspoon	onion powder
½ teaspoon	fine sea salt
1	egg
2 tablespoons	cornstarch
	honey mustard, for serving

Preheat oven to 400 degrees F. Drizzle the oil in a baking sheet, tilting to coat, and set aside.

In a small bowl, whisk together the honey, mustard, and mayonnaise in a small bowl and set aside.

Cut tenderloin widthwise in ½-inch slices. Cut each slice into 2- to 3-inch strips. In a shallow dish, whisk together breadcrumbs, paprika, onion powder, and salt. In a separate shallow dish, whisk the egg until well beaten.

Pour the cornstarch in a large ziplock bag. Add the pork strips and shake to coat. Dip each strip in the egg mixture and then the breading mixture. Arrange the pork strips on the baking sheet, leaving at least ½ inch between them. Bake, turning once halfway through cooking, until lightly browned and fully cooked, 14–16 minutes. Serve hot with honey mustard.

Glazed Pork Meatloaf

MAKES 4 SERVINGS

1 pound (85 percent lean)	ground pork
¼ cup	minced onion
2 cloves	garlic, minced
1	egg
¼ cup	Italian seasoned breadcrumbs
4 tablespoons	ketchup, divided
2 teaspoons	prepared yellow mustard
½ teaspoon	fine sea salt
½ teaspoon	freshly ground black pepper
2 tablespoons	barbecue sauce

Preheat oven to 350 degrees F. Line a baking sheet with aluminum foil and spray with nonstick cooking spray.

In a large bowl, combine the ground pork, onion, garlic, egg, breadcrumbs, 2 tablespoons of the ketchup, mustard, salt, and pepper. Mix until well blended, using hands if necessary. Pat into a loaf shape and transfer to the prepared baking sheet.

Bake for 30 minutes. Whisk together the remaining 2 tablespoons ketchup and barbecue sauce in a small bowl. Remove meatloaf from oven and brush with the glaze. Return to oven and continue baking until meatloaf is lightly browned and reaches an internal temperature of 160 degrees F, about 30 more minutes. Cool for 15 minutes and cut into slices.

Mississippi Pork Roast

MAKES 8 SERVINGS

1 (3-pound)	boneless pork roast, excess fat trimmed
½ teaspoon	freshly ground black pepper
2 tablespoons	extra-virgin olive oil
¼ cup	brine from a jar of pepperoncini peppers
½ packet (1 ounce)	ranch salad dressing mix
½ packet (1 ounce)	dry onion soup mix
½ cup (1 stick)	butter, cut into 8 pieces
10	pepperoncini peppers

Pat the roast dry with paper towels and sprinkle evenly with the black pepper. Heat the oil in a large frying pan over medium-high heat until it shimmers. Add the roast to the pan and sear it, turning occasionally with tongs, until it is browned on all sides, about 8 minutes.

Drain the roast on paper towels, then transfer to a large slow cooker. Drizzle with the pepperoncini brine. Sprinkle the ranch dressing mix and onion soup mix over roast. Arrange the butter pieces and pepperoncini peppers on top.

Cover and cook on low heat until the roast is very tender, about 8 hours.

Using two forks, shred and pull the meat apart, discarding any fatty pieces. Serve the pork accompanied with the cooking juices.

Best Sticky Glazed Ham
MAKES 12 SERVINGS

1 (8- to 10-pound)	bone-in fully cooked ham
½ cup	water
½ cup	butter
1 cup	dark brown sugar
½ cup	honey
2 tablespoons	Dijon mustard
1 teaspoon	garlic powder

Remove the ham from the refrigerator and trim off the hard rind, leaving the layer of fat. Let the ham sit at room temperature for 1 hour.

Arrange a rack in the lower third of the oven and preheat to 300 degrees F. Line a 9 x 13-inch baking dish with aluminum foil. Use a sharp knife to cut a scored 1-inch-wide diamond pattern on the fat layer of the ham, cutting about ¼ inch deep. Place the ham in the baking dish; pour the water into the base of the pan and cover with foil. Bake for 30 minutes.

Meanwhile, melt the butter in a small saucepan over medium heat. Add brown sugar, honey, mustard, and garlic powder, and stir until sugar dissolves and mixture simmers, about 4 minutes. Remove from heat and set aside.

Remove the ham from the oven and increase the oven temperature to 425 degrees F. Brush half of the glaze evenly over the ham. Return to the oven and bake uncovered for 20 minutes. Remove from oven, brush with the remaining glaze, and cook for 20 more minutes. Turn the broiler on high and broil the ham until golden brown, watching carefully so it doesn't burn, about 2 minutes. Remove from oven and rest for 20 minutes before cutting in slices.

Sheet-Pan Kielbasa and Potatoes

MAKES 6 SERVINGS

1 pound	Yukon Gold potatoes, peeled and cut into 1-inch pieces
2 tablespoons	Italian salad dressing,* divided
1 pound	smoked kielbasa, cut into ½-inch slices
1	small red bell pepper, seeded and diced
½	yellow onion, chopped
	kosher salt and freshly ground black pepper, to taste

Preheat oven to 350 degrees F and spray a rimmed baking sheet with nonstick cooking spray.

In a medium bowl, toss the potatoes with 1 tablespoon of the dressing. Transfer to the baking sheet and bake for 20 minutes.

Meanwhile, add the kielbasa, bell pepper, and onion to the bowl, drizzle with remaining 1 tablespoon dressing, and stir well. After potatoes have baked for 20 minutes, add the sausage mixture to the pan and stir to combine.

Increase the oven temperature to 450 degrees F. Return the pan to the oven and cook until potatoes are tender, 15–20 minutes. Sprinkle with salt and pepper and serve hot.

*Note: Use regular Italian dressing (not creamy or light) for best results.

BBQ Pork and Tater Bake

MAKES 6 SERVINGS

3 pounds	russet potatoes, peeled and cut into 2-inch pieces
6 ounces	cream cheese, softened
5 tablespoons	butter, softened
⅓ cup	milk
½ pound	bacon, cooked and crumbled
3 cups	shredded sharp cheddar cheese, divided
6 cups	pulled pork (see page 97)
	chopped chives or green onions, for garnish
	barbecue sauce, for serving

Preheat oven to 350 degrees F and lightly grease a 9 x 13-inch baking dish.

Fill a large pot with water and bring to a boil. Add the potatoes and cook, uncovered, until fork-tender, about 20 minutes. Drain and return to the pot.

Add the cream cheese and butter, and mash with a potato masher until the potatoes are mostly smooth with some smaller pieces remaining. Add the milk and stir to combine. Add the bacon and 2 cups of the cheddar cheese and stir well to combine.

Transfer potatoes to the prepared baking dish. Spoon the pulled pork evenly over the potatoes, and top with the remaining 1 cup cheese. Cover with aluminum foil and bake until hot and bubbling, about 30 minutes. Remove foil and bake for another 5 minutes or until cheese has fully melted and casserole is heated through. Garnish with chopped chives and serve with barbecue sauce on the side.

Pork Fried Rice

MAKES 4 SERVINGS

3 tablespoons	vegetable oil, divided
2	eggs, beaten
1	small yellow onion, finely chopped
$\frac{1}{2}$ pound	ground lean pork
1 teaspoon	kosher salt
$\frac{1}{4}$ teaspoon	freshly ground black pepper
2 cups	cold cooked white rice
$\frac{1}{2}$ cup	frozen peas and carrots mix
2 tablespoons	soy sauce or tamari
1 teaspoon	sesame oil

Heat 1 tablespoon oil in a wok or large nonstick frying pan over medium heat until shimmering. Add the eggs and cook, stirring occasionally with a spatula, until just set, about 2 minutes. Transfer to a bowl or plate and set aside.

Wipe out the frying pan, return it to the stove, and heat 1 tablespoon oil over medium heat. Add the onion and cook for 3 minutes. Add the pork, salt, and pepper. Continue cooking, breaking up the meat with a spatula, until the pork is cooked through and the onion is tender, about 5 minutes.

Add the remaining 1 tablespoon oil and heat for 30 seconds. Add the rice, peas and carrots, and soy sauce and cook, stirring frequently, until rice is hot, about 3 minutes. Add the eggs to the pan and cook until heated through. Drizzle with the sesame oil, give the mixture a quick stir, and serve hot.

#78

Bacon, Pork, and Parm Pasta

MAKES 6 SERVINGS

1 pound	sliced bacon, chopped
½ pound	lean pork loin, cut into ½-inch cubes
1	medium sweet onion, finely chopped
2 cloves	garlic, minced
¾ cup	chicken stock or broth
¾ cup	heavy cream
¼ teaspoon	fine sea salt
½ teaspoon	freshly ground black pepper
8 ounces	long fusilli pasta
1 cup	grated Parmesan cheese
	chopped parsley, for garnish

In a large frying pan over medium heat, cook the bacon until browned. Drain on paper towels and set aside. Pour out all but 1 tablespoon bacon drippings. Add the pork cubes and cook, stirring occasionally, until lightly browned and cooked through, about 8 minutes. Drain on paper towels.

Add the onion to the pan and cook over medium-low heat, stirring occasionally, until golden brown and caramelized, about 10 minutes. Add the garlic and cook, stirring, for 1 minute. Increase the heat to medium-high and add the chicken stock. Cook, stirring occasionally, until liquid reduces by half. Add the cream, salt, and pepper, and cook, stirring often, until sauce reduces and thickens. Add the pork and all but 2 tablespoons of the chopped bacon to the sauce. Stir to combine, lower heat, cover, and keep warm.

Heat a large pot of salted water over high heat until boiling. Add the pasta and cook according to package directions until al dente. Drain the pasta and add it to the sauce. Sprinkle the Parmesan cheese on top and stir to combine. Serve garnished with reserved bacon and chopped parsley.

#79

Perfect Pulled Pork

MAKES 8 SERVINGS

1 (about 4 pounds)	pork shoulder roast
1 cup	barbecue sauce
½ cup	apple cider vinegar
½ cup	beef stock or broth
¼ cup	packed dark brown sugar
1 tablespoon	Worcestershire sauce
1 tablespoon	prepared yellow mustard
1 tablespoon	chili powder
1	large yellow onion, chopped
3 cloves	garlic, minced

Place pork roast in a slow cooker, fat-side up. In a small bowl, whisk together the barbecue sauce, vinegar, beef stock, brown sugar, Worcestershire sauce, mustard, chili powder, onion, and garlic. Pour the mixture over the roast and cover. Cook on high temperature for 5–6 hours or low temperature for 8–10 hours, until pork is very tender and an instant read thermometer measures 195 to 205 degrees F.

Transfer pork from the slow cooker to a work surface and cool for 10–15 minutes. Use two forks to shred the meat, discarding any fat. Return shredded pork to the slow cooker, and stir to combine with juices.

Lemon Pork Medallions

MAKES 4 SERVINGS

1 (about 1 pound)	pork tenderloin
1 teaspoon	kosher salt
1 teaspoon	freshly ground black pepper
2 tablespoons	butter, divided
2 tablespoons	fresh lemon juice
1 teaspoon	Worcestershire sauce
1 teaspoon	Dijon mustard
	chopped fresh parsley, optional

Cut tenderloin into 8 even slices. Place each piece between
2 sheets of parchment paper, and use a rolling pin to flatten
each piece to a thickness of about ½ inch. Sprinkle both sides
with salt and pepper.

In a large frying pan over medium heat, melt 1 tablespoon
butter until it foams. Add the pork and cook, turning once,
until browned and an instant-read thermometer reads
145 degrees F, about 4 minutes per side. Transfer to a serving
plate and cover with aluminum foil.

Add remaining 1 tablespoon butter, lemon juice, Worcestershire
sauce, and mustard to the pan and heat, stirring to blend, just
until butter melts. Remove from heat, drizzle the sauce over
the pork, and sprinkle with parsley (if using) before serving.

Gala Apple Pork

MAKES 4 SERVINGS

4 tablespoons	packed brown sugar
½ teaspoon	ground cinnamon
⅛ teaspoon	fine sea salt
2	medium unpeeled Gala apples, cut into ½-inch slices
1 tablespoon	extra-virgin olive oil
4 (about ¾ inch thick)	bone-in pork rib chops, excess fat trimmed
	thyme sprigs, for garnish

Preheat oven to 350 degrees F and grease a 9 x 13-inch baking dish.

In a medium bowl, whisk together the brown sugar, cinnamon, and salt. Toss the apple slices in the mixture to coat. Transfer to the prepared baking dish, cover with aluminum foil, and bake for 15 minutes.

Heat the olive oil in a large frying pan over medium heat until it shimmers. Add the pork chops and cook, turning once, until lightly browned, 6–7 minutes.

Arrange the pork chops on top of the apples, cover with foil, and bake until pork is cooked through and measures 145 degrees F on an instant-read thermometer, 10–12 minutes. Divide among four plates and garnish pork with thyme sprigs.

Pork Spaghetti Bolognese

MAKES 8 SERVINGS

2 tablespoons	extra-virgin olive oil
1	medium yellow onion, finely chopped
4 cloves	garlic, minced
1	carrot, finely diced
1 stalk	celery, finely diced
1½ pounds	lean ground pork
1¼ cups	beef stock or broth
1 cup	whole milk
1 can (28 ounces)	whole Italian tomatoes, undrained
4 tablespoons	tomato paste
1 teaspoon	Italian seasoning
1	bay leaf
1 teaspoon	kosher salt
¼ teaspoon	freshly ground black pepper
1 pound	spaghetti
	grated Parmesan cheese, for sprinkling

In a large pot, heat the oil over medium heat until shimmering. Add onion and cook, stirring occasionally, until transparent, about 5 minutes. Add garlic, carrot, and celery, and cook until tender, about 5 minutes. Add the pork and cook, breaking up with a spatula, until cooked through, 6–8 minutes. Drain excess fat from the pot and return to the stove.

Add the beef stock and milk, increase heat to medium-high, and simmer until most of the liquid has evaporated, about 12 minutes.

Reduce heat to medium and add the tomatoes, tomato paste, Italian seasoning, bay leaf, salt, and pepper. Cook, breaking up tomatoes with a spoon, until mixture simmers. Cover and cook for 30 minutes.

Meanwhile, cook the spaghetti in a pot of boiling salted water, according to package directions. Drain and divide pasta among eight plates. Top with the sauce, removing the bay leaf, and sprinkle with Parmesan cheese.

#83

Orange and Honey Spiral Ham

MAKES 14 SERVINGS

1 (7- to 8-pound)	**spiral sliced ham**
1 cup	**packed brown sugar**
½ cup	**honey**
1 cup	**orange juice**

Unwrap ham and place flat-side down on a work surface. Rub the brown sugar all over the ham. Transfer to a large slow cooker, placing the flat side down. Drizzle the honey over the ham. Pour the orange juice in the slow cooker around the sides of the ham.

Cook on low temperature for 4 hours. Using tongs, carefully transfer the ham to a serving platter. Pour the cooking juices in a gravy boat and serve with the ham.

Tots-and-Brats Casserole

MAKES 4 SERVINGS

1 pound	cooked bratwurst links, cut into ½-inch diagonal slices
1	small onion, chopped
¼ teaspoon	fine sea salt
¼ teaspoon	freshly ground black pepper
1 pound	frozen Tater Tots, thawed
1 can (10 ¾ ounces)	condensed cream of mushroom soup
⅔ cup	milk
1 cup	shredded cheddar cheese

Preheat oven to 350 degrees F and lightly grease a 2-quart casserole dish.

Spray a large frying pan with nonstick cooking spray and heat over medium heat. Cook the bratwurst slices, turning once, until lightly browned, 6–7 minutes; drain on paper towels. Add the onion to the frying pan, sprinkle with salt and pepper, and cook, stirring occasionally, until transparent and tender, about 6 minutes.

Arrange bratwurst slices in prepared baking dish and sprinkle with cooked onion. Top with Tater Tots. In a small bowl, whisk together soup and milk. Pour mixture over Tater Tots and sprinkle with cheese. Bake, uncovered, for 30–40 minutes or until hot and bubbling.

Pork Egg Roll Bowl

MAKES 4 SERVINGS

1 tablespoon	extra-virgin olive oil
$\frac{1}{4}$ cup	chopped onion
3 cloves	garlic, minced
1 piece (2 inches)	fresh peeled ginger, grated
1 pound	lean ground pork
1 teaspoon	five-spice powder
2 tablespoons	soy sauce or tamari
5 cups	coleslaw mix or chopped cabbage
2	large carrots, peeled and grated
$3\frac{1}{2}$ cups	cooked long-grain rice
	finely chopped green onions, for garnish

Heat the oil in a large frying pan over medium heat until shimmering. Add the onion and cook until tender, about 5 minutes. Add the garlic and ginger and cook for 2 minutes.

Add the pork and cook, stirring occasionally and breaking meat apart with spatula, for 5 minutes. Sprinkle with the five-spice powder and drizzle with the soy sauce. Continue cooking until pork is cooked through and lightly browned. Add the coleslaw mix and carrots, and continue cooking, stirring frequently, until cabbage is tender, about 4 minutes. Serve mixture hot over rice and garnish with green onions.

Ham and Noodle Casserole

MAKES 6 SERVINGS

1 cup	whole milk
1 can (10 ounces)	condensed cream of mushroom soup
2 cups	shredded cheddar cheese
1 tub (6 ounces)	chive cream cheese, softened
½ teaspoon	kosher salt
½ teaspoon	freshly ground black pepper
8 ounces	egg noodles
2	large carrots, peeled and chopped
1 cup	frozen peas
2 cups	chopped ham
½ cup	panko crumbs

Preheat oven to 350 degrees F and grease a 9 x 13-inch glass baking dish.

In a large bowl, combine milk, soup, cheese, cream cheese, salt, and pepper and stir until smooth; set aside.

Fill a large pot with salted water and bring to a boil over high heat. Cook egg noodles for 2 minutes. Add carrots and cook for 2 minutes more. Add frozen peas and cook until water returns to a boil, about 2 more minutes. Drain well and add to the bowl with the cream cheese mixture. Add the ham and stir well to distribute ingredients.

Spread in the prepared baking dish, and top with panko crumbs. Cover with aluminum foil and bake until hot and bubbling, 30–35 minutes. Remove foil and continue baking until crumbs are lightly browned, about 10 more minutes. Cool for 10 minutes before serving.

SOUPS
&
STEWS

Sausage and Bacon Navy Bean Soup

MAKES 8–10 SERVINGS

1 pound	dried navy beans
4 1/2 cups	chicken stock or broth
1 can or bottle (12 ounces)	regular or nonalcoholic beer
1 can (15 ounces)	diced tomatoes, undrained
1	onion, chopped
2 stalks	celery, chopped
3 cloves	garlic, minced
1 pound	smoked sausage links, cut into 1/2-inch slices
2 tablespoons	Worcestershire sauce
1	bay leaf
8 strips	bacon, cooked and finely crumbled
	kosher salt and freshly ground black pepper, to taste
	chopped flat-leaf parsley, for garnish

Rinse and sort the beans. In a large pot, combine beans, stock, beer, tomatoes, onion, celery, garlic, sausage, Worcestershire sauce, and bay leaf; heat over medium-high until mixture comes to a boil. Lower heat, cover, and simmer for 4 hours, or until beans are tender, stirring occasionally and adding water if mixture becomes too thick. Stir in crumbled bacon and cook, stirring occasionally, for 10 minutes. Season with salt and pepper, and discard bay leaf before serving. Garnish with parsley.

Pork and Green Chile Stew
MAKES 6 SERVINGS

1 tablespoon	extra-virgin olive oil
1 pound	lean pork, cut into 1-inch cubes
1	medium onion, chopped fine
4 cloves	garlic, minced
1 teaspoon	ground cumin
1 teaspoon	dried oregano
1¼ pounds	roasted green chiles, peels and seeds removed, coarsely chopped
½	lime, juiced
2½ cups	chicken stock or broth
	kosher salt and freshly ground black pepper, to taste

Heat the oil in a Dutch oven or large saucepan over medium-high heat. Saute the pork until evenly browned, about 8 minutes. Using a slotted spoon, transfer to a paper towel to drain.

Return the pan to the heat and add the onion, garlic, cumin, and oregano. Cook, stirring often, until the onion just begins to brown, about 6 minutes. Add the green chiles and lime juice and cook, stirring often, for 5 minutes.

Return the browned pork cubes to the pan, add the chicken stock, and stir well. Reduce the heat to a simmer, cover, and cook for 1 hour, stirring occasionally. Season with salt and black pepper, cook for a few minutes more, and serve hot.

Pork Ramen Soup

MAKES 6 SERVINGS

6 cups	beef stock or broth
2 cloves	garlic, minced
2	medium boneless pork chops, fat trimmed, cut into 1/4-inch slices
2	thin carrots, peeled and cut into 1/4-inch diagonal slices
2 stalks	celery, cut into 1/2-inch diagonal slices
4 packages (3.5 ounces)	ramen noodles
1 cup	small broccoli florets
1/4 pound	snow peas, trimmed and cut into 1-inch diagonal slices
	kosher salt and freshly ground black pepper, to taste
	chopped green onions, for garnish
	tamari or soy sauce, for serving

Heat the stock in a large pot over medium-high heat until simmering. Add the garlic and stir. Add the pork and cook, stirring frequently, until cooked through, about 4 minutes. Use a slotted spoon to transfer the pork to a platter; tent with aluminum foil to keep warm.

Add the carrots to the hot broth and cook for 2 minutes. Add the celery and cook for 2 minutes. Add the noodles, breaking apart with a fork to separate, and cook until tender, about 4 minutes. Add the broccoli, snow peas, and pork, and cook for 1 more minute.

To serve, divide the noodles, vegetables, pork, and broth among six soup bowls. Sprinkle with salt and pepper, garnish with green onions, and serve with tamari on the side.

White Bean Ham Chowder

MAKES 10 SERVINGS

1 pound	dried great northern beans
1 pound	dried navy beans
7 quarts	water, divided
3 tablespoons	butter
3 cloves	garlic, minced
1	large onion, diced
2 stalks	celery, diced
1	medium carrot, peeled and diced
1	ham bone
8 ounces	thick-sliced ham, chopped
2 teaspoons	kosher salt
1 teaspoon	freshly ground black pepper
$\frac{1}{2}$ teaspoon	dried thyme

Rinse and sort the beans. Pour 4 quarts water into a large stockpot and add the beans. Bring to a boil over high heat. Remove from the burner, cover, and let stand 1 hour. Drain the beans and discard the soaking water; set aside the drained beans.

Dry the pot, add the butter, and melt over medium-high heat until it foams. Add garlic and cook for 1 minute. Add the onion, celery, and carrot and cook for 5 minutes, stirring occasionally. Add the remaining 3 quarts water, ham bone, and beans. Bring to boil, reduce heat to low, cover, and cook until beans are tender, 3–4 hours. (Cooking time may vary depending on the moisture content of the beans.)

Add the chopped ham, salt, pepper, and thyme. Cook uncovered for 30 minutes. Remove ham bone and serve.

High-on-the Hog Jambalaya
MAKES 6 SERVINGS

4 strips	bacon, chopped
1 pound	smoked sausage, cut into ½-inch cubes
1	large onion, chopped
¾ cup	diced green bell pepper
½ cup	diced celery
1 teaspoon	Cajun seasoning
1 cup	uncooked long-grain white rice
1 can (14.5 ounces)	whole tomatoes, chopped and juice reserved
2 cloves	garlic, minced
2 cups	chicken broth
1 cup	diced cooked ham
¼ teaspoon	dried thyme
1	bay leaf
	kosher salt and freshly ground black pepper, to taste
2 tablespoons	chopped flat-leaf parsley, for garnish

Add the bacon to a Dutch oven or large pot and cook over medium heat, stirring occasionally, until fat begins to render and bacon is lightly browned, about 7 minutes. Stir in sausage and cook, stirring occasionally, for 5 minutes. Add the onion, bell pepper, and celery, and cook and stir until tender, 7–8 minutes.

Stir in the Cajun seasoning, rice, tomatoes with their juices, garlic, broth, ham, thyme, and bay leaf. Bring to a simmer over medium-high heat, then reduce heat to medium-low, cover, and simmer 30 minutes or until rice is tender. Season with salt and pepper.

Remove the pot from the heat, discard bay leaf, and let stand 5 minutes. Garnish with parsley before serving.

Smoked Sausage Split Pea Soup
MAKES 8 SERVINGS

2 cups	dried split peas
4 cups	water
4 cups	chicken stock or broth
1 pound	smoked sausage, cut into ¼-inch slices
1	large onion, chopped
2 cloves	garlic, minced
pinch	dried thyme
3 stalks	celery, chopped
3	carrots, chopped
	kosher salt and freshly ground black pepper, to taste
	chopped chives, for garnish

In a stock pot, combine dried peas with water and stock. Bring to a simmer over medium-high heat. Remove from the heat, cover, and let sit for 1 hour.

Cut the sausage slices in quarters. In a large frying pan over medium heat, cook the sausage, turning occasionally, until browned, about 8 minutes. Drain on paper towels and add to the split pea mixture. Return the frying pan to the stove and add the onion to the drippings. Cook, stirring occasionally, until tender, about 5 more minutes. Add the onion to the pea mixture along with the garlic and thyme, and heat over medium-high heat until simmering. Cover, reduce heat to low, and simmer for 1½ hours, stirring occasionally.

Add celery and carrots to the pot, increase heat to medium, and cook, uncovered, until carrots are tender, about 40 minutes. Season with salt and pepper and serve garnished with chopped chives.

Polish Sausage Cabbage Chowder

MAKES 8 SERVINGS

2 tablespoons	extra-virgin olive oil
1 pound	smoked Polish sausage links, cut into $\frac{1}{4}$-inch slices
2	medium carrots, peeled and cut into $\frac{1}{4}$-inch slices
1	small onion, diced
1	small green cabbage, cut into 1-inch pieces
2	medium leeks, white and pale green parts only, cut into $\frac{1}{4}$-inch slices
2 stalks	celery, diced
2 cloves	garlic, minced
6 cups	chicken or vegetable stock
1 pound	red potatoes, diced
1	bay leaf
	kosher salt and freshly ground black pepper, to taste

Heat the oil in a Dutch oven or large pot over medium heat. Add sausage slices and cook, turning once, until browned, 7–8 minutes. Drain on paper towels and set aside.

Add carrots and onion to the drippings in pot and cook for 5 minutes, stirring occasionally. Add cabbage, leeks, and celery and cook until tender, about 6 minutes. Add garlic and cook until fragrant, 1–2 minutes.

Add stock, potatoes, bay leaf, and browned sausage and stir to combine. Bring soup to a boil, then reduce heat to medium-low, cover, and simmer until potatoes are tender, 15–20 minutes. Discard bay leaf. Season with salt and pepper, ladle into bowls, and serve.

Cowgirl Stew
MAKES 10 SERVINGS

6 strips	bacon, chopped
1 cup	chopped onion
2 (1-pound)	boneless pork chops, trimmed and cut into 1/2-inch cubes
3 cloves	garlic, minced
1/4 cup	flour
1 tablespoon	chili powder
1 teaspoon	paprika
1 teaspoon	cumin
1 teaspoon	fine sea salt
1/2 teaspoon	freshly ground black pepper
1 can (14 1/2 ounces)	diced tomatoes, undrained
1 can (15 1/2 ounces)	whole kernel corn, drained
1 can (10 ounces)	diced tomatoes and green chiles, undrained
1 can (15 ounces)	chili beans, undrained
3	large red potatoes, cubed
12 ounces	smoked sausage, chopped
1 cup	beef stock or broth
1 tablespoon	chopped parsley, for garnish

In a Dutch oven over medium heat, cook bacon, stirring occasionally, until crispy, 8–10 minutes. Drain on paper towels, crumble, and set aside. Drain all but 2 tablespoons of the pan drippings. Add the onion and cook over medium heat until tender, 4–5 minutes. Add the pork and cook, stirring occasionally, until lightly browned, 8–9 minutes. Add the garlic and cook for 1 more minute.

Sprinkle with flour, chili powder, paprika, cumin, salt, and pepper, and cook, stirring, for 1 minute. Add the tomatoes, corn, tomatoes and green chiles, chili beans, potatoes, sausage, and stock. Bring to a simmer and cover. Cook until potatoes are tender, 20–25 minutes. Serve the stew in warmed soup bowls and garnish with bacon and parsley.

Sausage, Bean, and Kale Soup
MAKES 8 SERVINGS

1 pound	bulk spicy Italian sausage
1 cup	onion, diced
3 cloves	garlic, minced
2	large carrots, peeled and diced
2 stalks	celery, diced
2 cans (15 ounces each)	white beans, drained and rinsed
4 cups	chicken stock or broth
1 teaspoon	Italian seasoning
2 cups	chopped kale
	kosher salt and freshly ground black pepper, to taste
⅓ cup	grated Parmesan cheese
1 tablespoon	chopped fresh parsley, for garnish

In a large stockpot over medium heat, cook the sausage until browned, breaking it apart with a spatula as it cooks, 5–6 minutes. Add the onion, garlic, carrots, and celery, and cook, stirring occasionally, until onion is translucent, about 5 minutes.

Add the beans, stock, and Italian seasoning. Simmer over medium heat for 30 minutes. Add the kale and cook until crisp-tender, about 5 minutes. Season with salt and pepper. Serve soup in warmed bowls and sprinkle with Parmesan cheese and parsley.

Chorizo Spanish Rice Soup

MAKES 6 SERVINGS

2 tablespoons	extra-virgin olive oil
1 pound	link or bulk chorizo
1	medium green bell pepper, diced
1	medium onion, diced
1 can (10 ounces)	diced tomatoes and green chiles, undrained
5 cups	beef stock or broth
1 can (15 ounces)	tomato sauce
1 package (5.6 ounces)	Spanish rice mix
1/3 cup	sour cream
1/2 cup	shredded Mexican blend cheese

Heat the oil in a large pan over medium heat. If using link chorizo, remove casings. Cook the sausage for 5 minutes, breaking up with spatula, and add bell pepper and onion. Continue cooking, stirring occasionally, until onion is translucent and bell pepper is tender, 8–10 minutes.

Add the diced tomatoes and chiles, beef stock, tomato sauce, and Spanish rice mix to the pot. Increase heat to medium-high and bring to a boil. Reduce heat to medium-low, cover, and simmer until rice is tender, 20–25 minutes. Ladle into bowls and garnish with a dollop of sour cream, stirring once gently with a small spoon to swirl, and sprinkle with cheese.

Easy Slow-Cooker Posole
MAKES 8 SERVINGS

2 pounds	pork sirloin roast, cut into 1-inch cubes
2 teaspoons	kosher salt
1/2 teaspoon	freshly ground black pepper
3 tablespoons	extra-virgin olive oil
1	medium yellow onion, chopped
4 cloves	garlic, minced
1 can (19 ounces)	red enchilada sauce
1 jar (16 ounces)	salsa verde
2 cups	chicken stock or broth
1 can (4 ounces)	chopped green chiles
2 cans (15.5 ounces each)	white hominy, drained
2 teaspoons	dried oregano
1/2 teaspoon	fine sea salt
1/2 teaspoon	cayenne pepper
	lime wedges, chopped cilantro, and chopped red onion, for serving

Season the pork on all sides with kosher salt and pepper. In a large frying pan, heat the oil over medium-high heat until shimmering. Add the pork and cook, stirring occasionally, until browned on all sides, 6–8 minutes. Transfer the meat to a 6-quart slow cooker.

Return the frying pan to the stove and add the onion. Cook, stirring often, until onion is translucent, about 5 minutes. Add garlic and cook for 1 more minute. Add mixture to slow cooker. Add the enchilada sauce, salsa verde, stock, chiles, hominy, oregano, fine sea salt, and cayenne pepper to the slow cooker, and stir to combine. Cover and cook on high for 6–7 hours (or low for 8–9 hours) until the pork is very tender. Serve with lime wedges, chopped cilantro, and red onion.

Lasagna Soup

MAKES 6 SERVINGS

1 pound	sweet or spicy Italian sausage (links or bulk)
1	large sweet onion, chopped
2 cloves	garlic, minced
1/4 cup	tomato paste
1 (28-ounce)	can whole peeled tomatoes (preferably San Marzano), chopped and juices reserved
4 cups	chicken or vegetable stock
1 tablespoon	chopped fresh oregano or 1 teaspoon dried
1 teaspoon	fine sea salt
1 teaspoon	freshly ground black pepper
4 ounces	curly lasagna noodles, broken into bite-size pieces
1/2 cup	shredded mozzarella cheese
1/2 cup	grated Parmesan cheese
12	fresh basil leaves, chopped

If using sausage links, remove casings. Crumble sausage in a Dutch oven or large pot, add onion, and cook over medium heat, breaking up the meat with a spatula, until sausage is browned and onion is translucent, 8–10 minutes. Drain any excess grease. Add garlic and cook until fragrant, 1–2 minutes. Add tomato paste and stir until well distributed.

Add tomatoes and juices, stock, oregano, salt, and pepper. Bring to a boil, add the noodles and cook until al dente, 12–14 minutes, stirring occasionally. Sprinkle in the mozzarella and Parmesan cheeses, stir until mozzarella just starts to melt, and ladle into bowls. Sprinkle with basil and serve.

Cheesy Kielbasa Potato Soup
MAKES 6 SERVINGS

2	medium Yukon Gold potatoes, peeled and cut into $\frac{1}{2}$-inch dice
1 pound	kielbasa, cut into $\frac{1}{2}$-inch slices
1	medium yellow onion, diced
4 $\frac{1}{2}$ cups	chicken stock or broth
$\frac{1}{2}$ teaspoon	fine sea salt
$\frac{1}{4}$ teaspoon	cayenne pepper
$\frac{1}{4}$ teaspoon	black pepper
1 cup	half-and-half
2 cups	shredded sharp cheddar cheese finely chopped flat-leaf parsley, for garnish

In a medium pot, cover the potatoes with 2 inches of cold water and bring to a boil. Cook potatoes until just barely tender, about 8 minutes. Drain and set aside.

While potatoes are cooking, cut the kielbasa slices in half. In a Dutch oven or large pot, cook the kielbasa and onion over medium heat until kielbasa is lightly browned and onion is translucent, 8–10 minutes. Using tongs, remove 6 kielbasa slices to a paper towel and drain. Chop finely for garnish and set aside.

Drain any excess grease and add the chicken stock, potatoes, salt, cayenne pepper, and black pepper. Bring to a gentle boil and cook until potatoes are tender.

Add half-and-half and heat until simmering. Add the cheese and cook, stirring constantly, just until cheese melts. Ladle into bowls, garnish with reserved chopped sausage and parsley, and serve.

#100
Grandma's Pork Stew
MAKES 8–10 SERVINGS

2 pounds	pork sirloin roast, cut into 1-inch cubes
2 teaspoons	kosher salt
1/2 teaspoon	freshly ground black pepper
3 tablespoons	extra-virgin olive oil
3	medium carrots, peeled and cut into 1/2-inch dice
1	large yellow onion, chopped
2 cloves	garlic, minced
2	medium Yukon Gold potatoes, peeled and cut into 1-inch dice
3 cups	chicken stock or broth
1/2 cup	tomato sauce
1 teaspoon	Worcestershire sauce
1 teaspoon	fresh thyme, minced
1/2 cup	frozen peas
	chopped flat-leaf parsley, for garnish

Season the pork on all sides with salt and pepper. In a large heavy pot or Dutch oven, heat the oil over medium-high heat until shimmering. Add the pork and cook, stirring occasionally, until browned on all sides, 6–8 minutes. Transfer to paper towels to drain.

Add carrots and onion to the pot. Cook, stirring often, until onion is tender, about 5 minutes. Add garlic and cook for 1 more minute. Stir in pork, potatoes, stock, tomato sauce, Worcestershire sauce, and thyme. Increase heat to medium-high. Bring to a boil, reduce heat to medium-low, cover, and simmer until potatoes are tender, about 25 minutes. Add peas and cook until tender, about 5 minutes. Garnish with parsley.

Pasta e Fagioli Soup

MAKES 6 SERVINGS

¼ pound	bacon, diced
1	carrot, peeled and diced
1 stalk	celery, diced
1	medium onion, diced
2 cloves	garlic, minced
1 can (14 ounces)	crushed San Marzano tomatoes
1 can (15 ounces)	kidney beans, drained and rinsed
1 can (15 ounces)	cannellini beans, drained and rinsed
6 cups	chicken stock or broth
2 teaspoons	fresh chopped thyme
½ pound	ditalini pasta or macaroni
	kosher salt and freshly ground black pepper, to taste
1 tablespoon	chopped fresh parsley, for garnish
¼ cup	grated Parmesan cheese, for garnish

In a large frying pan over medium heat, cook the bacon, stirring occasionally, until just starting to brown, 7–8 minutes. Add the carrot, celery, and onion and continue cooking until onion is translucent, about 5 minutes. Add the garlic and cook for 1 more minute. Add the tomatoes, beans, stock, and thyme.

Increase the heat to medium-high and bring to a boil. Reduce heat to medium-low and simmer uncovered for 15 minutes. Add the pasta and continue cooking, stirring occasionally, until pasta is al dente, about 15 minutes. Season with salt and pepper. Serve garnished with parsley and Parmesan cheese.

NOTES

NOTES

NOTES

Metric Conversion Chart

VOLUME MEASUREMENTS		WEIGHT MEASUREMENTS		TEMPERATURE CONVERSION	
U.S.	Metric	U.S.	Metric	Fahrenheit	Celsius
1 teaspoon	5 ml	½ ounce	15 g	250	120
1 tablespoon	15 ml	1 ounce	30 g	300	150
¼ cup	60 ml	3 ounces	90 g	325	160
⅓ cup	75 ml	4 ounces	115 g	350	180
½ cup	125 ml	8 ounces	225 g	375	190
⅔ cup	150 ml	12 ounces	350 g	400	200
¾ cup	175 ml	1 pound	450 g	425	220
1 cup	250 ml	2¼ pounds	1 kg	450	230

MORE 101 THINGS® IN THESE

FAVORITES

AIR FRYER	GRITS
BACON	INSTANT POT®
BBQ	POTATO
CASSEROLE	RAMEN NOODLES
CHICKEN	SLOW COOKER
CHOCOLATE	SMOKER
DUTCH OVEN	TORTILLA

Each 128 pages, $12.99

Available at bookstores or directly from Gibbs Smith
1.800.835.4993
www.gibbs-smith.com

Gibbs Smith

About the Author

Eliza Cross is an award-winning author and food blogger. She is the founder of the BENSA Bacon Lovers Society, and an E.A.T. Certified Culinary Judge. She lives with her family in Denver, Colorado.